UNIX PROGRAMMING

Unix Programming

Editor:

Dr. Jovan Pehcevski, Ph.D.

ArclerPress

www.arclerpress.com

Unix Programming
Editor: Dr. Jovan Pehcevski, Ph.D.

708 3rd Avenue, 6th Floor
New York
NY 10017
United States of America
www.arclerpress.com

ISBN: 978-1-68094-450-1

Library of Congress Control Number: 2016951140

About the Editor

Dr. Jovan Pehcevski, Ph.D.

Jovan obtained his PhD in Computer Science from RMIT University in Melbourne, Australia in 2007. His research interests include big data, business intelligence and predictive analytics, data and information science, information retrieval, XML, web services and service-oriented architectures, and relational and NoSQL database systems. He has published over 30 journal and conference papers and he also serves as a journal and conference reviewer. He is currently working as a Dean and Associate Professor at European University in Skopje, Macedonia.

Contents

List of Contributors

Mark Burgess

Centre of Science and Technology Faculty of Engineering, Oslo College

Preface

UNIX, like other operating systems, has two primary functions: to manage the operations of the hardware and to manage the running of the applications. The UNIX system includes traditional components of the operating system, plus a set of libraries and a set of bundled applications. On the lowest, hardware level there are two components: the file system and the process control. On the intermediary level there is the set of programming libraries, while on the upper level there are the applications.

The part of the UNIX operating system that manages the hardware and the processes is called the kernel. To enable control over the hardware devices, the UNIX system treats each device as a file (named device file). This allows for any hardware device to be accessed much like accessing the files in the system. The file system therefore manages read and/or write access to both user data and devices (such as a printer) connected to the computer. During process execution, UNIX allocates resources to processes (including the CPU, the disk, and the memory) and mediates the access to the hardware.

A significant advantage of UNIX over other operating systems is its application portability, i.e. the ability to have an application executed on various types of computer hardware, without the need to modify it. This allows the programmer to develop software that, with minimal effort, will execute on different types of hardware. In this way, the application development costs are reduced and the number of potential application uses is increased.

This edition is dedicated to the UNIX programming, which is basically done in the standard C language (BSD C library), that exists for almost 50 years.

Section 1 explains the basic concepts of the UNIX operating system, such as the kernel, the file system, and the processes.

Section 2 covers the basic programming techniques that involve input and output operations (stdin, stdout, stderr), shell scripts, compiling and linking (gcc), the Makefile option, and using standard programming libraries.

Section 3 goes into intermediary topics in UNIX programming and covers file access and manipulation, such as file descriptors, read/write/seek functions, file properties (stat, fstat, lstat), user privileges, processes (main, fork, exit), pipes and fifos, domain sockets and memory access.

Section 4 covers advanced topics in UNIX programming dedicated on network programming (bind, connect, listen, send, receive, accept, close) and multithread programming, such as synchronization, pthread_create, pthread_exit, and pthread_join.

Editor

Dr. Jovan Pehcevski, Ph.D.

INTRODUCTION

UNIX is a computer operating system - the base software that controls a computer system and its peripherals. In this sense, UNIX behaves in the same way that the perhaps more familiar PC operating systems Windows or MacOS behave. It provides the base mechanisms for booting a computer, logging in, running applications, storing and retrieving files, etc.

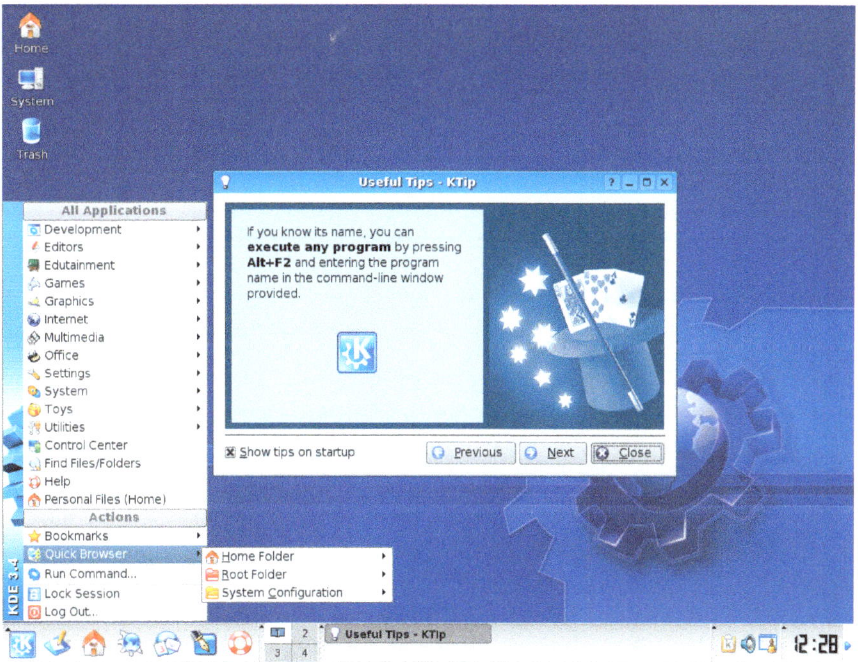

More specifically, the word "UNIX" refers to a family of operating systems that are related to one or both of the original UNIX operating systems - BSD and SystemV. Examples of modern UNIX operating systems include IRIX (from SGI), Solaris (from Sun), Tru64 (from Compaq) and Linux (from the Free Software community). Even though these different "flavors" of UNIX have unique characteristics and come from different sources, they all work alike in a number of fundamental ways. If you gain familiarity with any one of these UNIX-based operating systems, you will also have gained at least some familiarity with nearly every other variant of UNIX.

UNIX has been around for a long time (over 30 years). It predates the concept of the personal computer. As such, it was designed from the ground up to be a multi-user, shared, networked operating environment. UNIX has concepts such as Users, Groups, Permissions and Network-Shared Resources (such as files, printers, other computer systems, etc.) built-in to the core of its design. This makes UNIX a uniquely powerful and flexible operating system. Along with this power and flexibility comes some unique concepts that make UNIX what it is. These concepts are relatively simple and should be understood to take full advantage of the operating system.

Users: In order to make use of a UNIX system, you must first log in. This requires a user account, which consists of:

- Username: This is your login name and is how you are identified to the system itself and to other users of the system.
- Password: Along with your username, your password grants you access to the system. Don't forget or lose your password. If you write your password down, keep it in a safe place.
- Default group: The default group that your username belongs to (see Groups below).
- Contact info: So that system administrators and other users can contact you if necessary.
- Home directory: A directory or "folder" assigned to your username. This grants you access to disk storage. This is where you will keep your files and data.
- Default shell: The program which manages your login and command line sessions.

Groups: A UNIX group is a collection of users - i.e. a list of usernames. Groups provide a mechanism to assign permissions (see below) to a list of users all at once. For our purposes, group associations are typically based on which research group or area of study a user is affiliated with. Each user can belong to more than one group.

Permissions: Everything in UNIX is "owned" by both a user and a group. The simplest example of this would be files (but this concept is not limited only to files). By manipulating permissions, the user who owns a file can define which other users and groups can read or modify that file. In this way, users can secure sensitive files from prying eyes and keep themselves or others from accidentially deleting important data.

Shared Resources: UNIX is a networked operating environment at its core. As such, nearly everything that one can access on the local system can also be accessed via the network from remote systems. This includes, among other possibilities, editing and sharing files, running software, or using printers. Even the contents of a UNIX system's display can be manipulated remotely.

The actions that an individual user is able to perform remotely is defined by the permissions assigned to that user (or any group to which the user belongs) for each of these activities.

UNIX Processes

When a program is started on UNIX, it creates what is known as a "process" on the system. Every process is assigned a unique serial number called its process id or PID for short. Processes can be created by any user, but can only be destroyed by someone with the permissions to do so - usually the user that created the process or the system administrator. This ensures that the compute jobs you start on the system will not be disturbed by any other user of the system until they complete or you decide to stop them yourself.

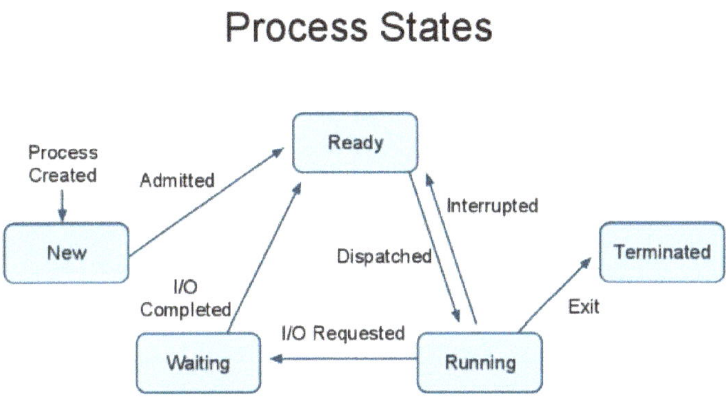

Processes and process management becomes important on UNIX systems that are shared between a number of users. The concept of users and PIDs is the main tool by which the available system resources are shared fairly among everybody who needs access to them. Processes can be suspended or given lower priority in cases where one or more users should step out of the way for someone else, but wish to do so without losing their work up to that point.

One further consideration on this topic is the fact that a running UNIX process can spawn "child" processes. For example, any program you run from inside a UNIX shell will be a child process of that shell. Conversely, the shell is the parent process of this child. Child proceses have associated with them both their own process id (PID) as well as their parent's process id (PPID).

Normally this concept of parent and child processes is not something you need to be bothered with as a user. However, it can be useful to understand how UNIX organizes processes if you are trying to keep track of certain system resources (e.g. memory and CPU), if you are working with environment variables, or if you need to track down a rogue program or script.

Obtaining a user Account

As already mentioned, before you can do anything on a UNIX system you must have a user account. This is usually obtained by introducing yourself to your friendly neighborhood system administrator and asking them to create an account for you. If you make a good impression, you will be asked for some information and the account will be created within a matter of minutes.

Logging in

Once you have been given a user account, you can get started. The first step is to log in by providing a valid username and password to the system. This will grant you some level of access to the system depending on how you log in. There are essentially two types of logins: console (local) logins and remote logins:

Console login:

In the practical sense, the term "console" is just a fancy word for the display and input devices that are directly attached to a UNIX system. Logging in at the console means that you are physically sitting at the machine and will log in via the mouse, keyboard, and display that are attached to the system.

When you sit at the console, you should see the login window on the screen (if the screen is blank, move the mouse or press the shift key on the keyboard to wake up the display). The exact details of the login window will vary between the different flavors of UNIX, but at the very least you will see a place to enter your username. Note: Some systems may require you to point your mouse over the login window before the keyboard is activated in that window.

1. Type your username at the appropriate place in the login window

2. Press "enter" to bring you to the password field (Note: Some systems may require you to press "tab" to move to the password field).

3. Type your password into the password field. You will not see your password as it is being typed, so type carefully. Also keep in mind that UNIX systems are case-sensitive. That means that if your password is "ImaDork3", you must type exactly "ImaDork3" to preserve the pattern of lower case and capital letters. "imadork3" and "IMADORK3" would be completely different passwords to UNIX.

4. Once you've typed your password, press enter (or click the appropriate action button if present on the login window). If you've typed everything correctly, you will be granted access. The login screen will disappear and be replaced with the system's Graphical User Interface or "GUI" (covered in the next part of this introduction).

Once you have completed these steps, your user is the "owner" of the console. As such, you have control over the input devices, the display, and its contents. Remote users or systems will be unable to access any of these resources without your permission.

Remote login

UNIX is a multi-user networked operating system. As such, you are able to log in to remote systems and do work right alongside other users without leaving your office or kicking the other users off (you do, however, have to remember that you are sharing system resources with all the users who are currently logged on).

Remote logins are also known as "shell access". We will talk more about the UNIX shell later, but for now just keep in mind that the shell is a place where you give instructions to a UNIX system (like starting a program or deleting a file) via a command-line interface. When performing a remote login, it is assumed that you are already logged in to the console of a local UNIX machine (or perhaps a PC) and wish to gain shell access on a remote UNIX machine.

In order to proceed, you should know the fully qualified domain name of the system you wish to remotely log in to. The fully qualified domain name is a combination of the hostname and the domain name of a system. Every properly configured UNIX system has both a hostname and a domain name.

1. Start a UNIX shell (covered later) and make that window active.

2. You will now use a program called "ssh" (short for "Secure SHell") to log in to the remote system. At the shell prompt (%), you would type, for example:

   % ssh jake@reef.structbio.vanderbilt.edu

   and press enter. In the example above, you would be connected to the system with hostname "reef" in the domain "structbio.vanderbilt.edu" as user "jake".

   Systems in structural biology have a domain name of "structbio.vanderbilt.edu". Often, you will be connecting between machines that reside in the same domain. In this case the domain name can usually be left off. For example, if you were on a system in the domain "structbio.vanderbilt.edu" and wanted to remotely log in to the machine called "reef" you could type:

   % ssh jake@reef

   or if your username is the same on both machines you can leave out that part, too:

   % ssh reef

3. In any case, ssh will connect to the system reef.structbio.vanderbilt.edu and ask for user jake's password. Type the password (remember about case-sensitivity) and press enter. If you were successful, a shell will be started for you on the remote system and you will get a command prompt. You can now give the remote system commands via the remote shell's command-line interface.

Graphical User Interfaces in UNIX

It is important to recognize that in UNIX the GUI is separate from the operating system itself. This is unlike Windows or MacOS9 and earlier which won't run without the GUI (or at the very least are extremely crippled if you do so). The GUI on UNIX is a separate layer that sits on top of the core operating system. In principle, you can uninstall the GUI and still have a completely functional UNIX system sans any graphical programs.

The X Window System

Version 11 of something called the X Window System is the underlying graphics layer on all modern UNIX systems (Except for MacOSX where it is an optional add-on). "X Windows", or just "X11" or "X" as it is commonly called, provides the glue between the underlying operating system, graphical applications, and graphics hardware. There are many thousands of software applications written for the X window system.

X by itself is not a GUI. Rather, X provides the facilities that a GUI requires - namely the ability to accept input from devices like a mouse and keyboard, and the ability to draw graphical objects to a computer display. So, despite its name, the X Window System cannot draw "windows", at least not by the modern definition of "window". This is the job of another piece of software called the window manager. There are many different window managers available for X. Some of these are proprietary and will only run on a particular type of UNIX. Some of these are open and will run on any system that has X installed.

Getting to Know X

The X Window System has some very unique and useful features. These things are provided by X itself and as such are common to all X window managers and all UNIX/ X_{11} systems:

Copying and pasting text

You may have noticed that in addition to the typical left and right mouse buttons, your UNIX workstation also sports a middle mouse button. Here is why: Most X applications allow you to highlight text with the left mouse button, making this text immediately available to be pasted to a new location. To paste the highlighted text, place the mouse in the new location and single-click the middle button. This is an extremely useful and time-saving technique, especially when working at the command line.

Note: In order to paste text, it must remain selected. Once a selection has been de-activated (usually by left-clicking inside of selectable area) the current selection is "forgotten" and is no longer available to X.

Displaying a remote program locally

This is perhaps the most useful and powerful feature of the X window system. X is a "client-server" environment. The way to think of this is the following: Every X program is a client, and every X display device is a server. Any X application (client) can display its contents over the network to any X display (server) as long as the permissions on the X server allow it. What does this mean? You can log in to a remote machine, run an

X application, and have the application's contents show up on the console of the local system.

There are typically five steps to this:

1. Login to the console of an X Windows system. For this example, we will assume the console machine's name is "moray.structbio.vanderbilt.edu". This is where your X applications will be displayed .

2. Start two UNIX shells. Use the first one to remotely log in to another system (See part 2 for an example). For this example, we will assume the remote machine's name is reef.structbio.vanderbilt.edu

3. Once you are on the machine reef, set your DISPLAY environment variable to moray's default display:

   reef% setenv DISPLAY moray.structbio.vanderbilt.edu:0

4. In the second UNIX shell on moray, give reef permission to write to moray's X server:

   moray% xhost +reef.structbio.vanderbilt.edu

5. Run an X application on reef. The application will run on reef, but it's graphical output will be output over the network to moray's X server:

   reef% xterm &

You will now have the program xterm running on reef, but displaying on moray.

Note 1: In some instances, the ssh program will automatically set up the X network connection for you. In these cases, you can skip the "setenv DISPLAY" and "xhost" commands (steps 3 and 4 above).

Note 2: You are not limited to one remote X connection. You can have multiple remote applications from multiple remote machines simultaneously running and displaying their contents onto a single console's display.

Useful X programs

As mentioned above, there are thousands of X applications. There are a few useful X programs distributed as part of the standard X Window System distribution, and should be available on all machines which have a copy of X installed. Here is a partial listing of these:

- Xhost: sets permissions for the console's X display
- xdpyinfo - reports lots of useful technical information about the console's X display
- xterm - a terminal program for X (UNIX shell)
- xcalc - a graphical calculator

- xclock - a graphical clock
- xeyes - a cute program to help keep track of your mouse pointer
- xfontsel - a font browser
- xman - a graphical manual page viewer
- xset - sets various parameters such as keyboard repeat rate, system bell volume, and screen blank timings.

SECTION I: UNIX BASIC CONCEPTS

1
CHAPTER

UNIX BASIC CONCEPTS

UNIX INTRODUCTION

This section concerns UNIX, which is a common operating system. By operating system, we mean the suite of programs which make the computer work. UNIX is used by the workstations and multi-user servers within the school.

On X terminals and the workstations, X Windows provide a graphical interface between the user and UNIX. However, knowledge of UNIX is required for operations which aren't covered by a graphical program, or for when there is no X windows system, for example, in a telnet session.

The UNIX operating system

The UNIX operating system is made up of three parts; the kernel, the shell and the programs.

The kernel

The kernel of UNIX is the hub of the operating system: it allocates time and memory to programs and handles the filestore and communications in response to system calls.

As an illustration of the way that the shell and the kernel work together, suppose a user types rm myfile (which has the effect of removing the file **myfile**). The shell searches the filestore for the file containing the program rm, and then requests the kernel, through system calls, to execute the program rm on myfile. When the process rm myfile has finished running, the shell then returns the UNIX prompt % to the user, indicating that it is waiting for further commands.

Citation: "UNIX Tutorial for Beginners", web tutorial by Open of Course Initiative, 2014

The shell

The shell acts as an interface between the user and the kernel. When a user logs in, the login program checks the username and password, and then starts another program called the shell. The shell is a command line interpreter (CLI). It interprets the commands the user types in and arranges for them to be carried out. The commands are themselves programs: when they terminate, the shell gives the user another prompt (% on our systems).

The adept user can customise his/her own shell, and users can use different shells on the same machine. Staff and students in the school have the tcsh shell by default.

The tcsh shell has certain features to help the user inputting commands.

Filename Completion - By typing part of the name of a command, filename or directory and pressing the [Tab] key, the tcsh shell will complete the rest of the name automatically. If the shell finds more than one name beginning with those letters you have typed, it will beep, prompting you to type a few more letters before pressing the tab key again.

History - The shell keeps a list of the commands you have typed in. If you need to repeat a command, use the cursor keys to scroll up and down the list or type history for a list of previous commands.

Files and Processes

Everything in UNIX is either a file or a process.

A process is an executing program identified by a unique PID (process identifier).

A file is a collection of data. They are created by users using text editors, running compilers etc.

Examples of files:

- a document (report, essay etc.)
- the text of a program written in some high-level programming language
- instructions comprehensible directly to the machine and incomprehensible to a casual user, for example, a collection of binary digits (an executable or binary file);
- a directory, containing information about its contents, which may be a mixture of other directories (subdirectories) and ordinary files.

THE DIRECTORY STRUCTURE

All the files are grouped together in the directory structure. The file-system is arranged in a hierarchical structure, like an inverted tree. The top of the hierarchy is traditionally called **root**.

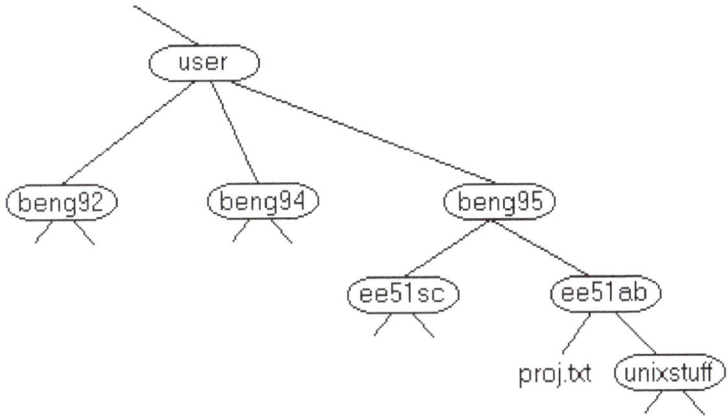

In the diagram above, we see that the directory ee51ab contains the subdirectory unixstuff and a file proj.txt

STARTING AN XTERMINAL SESSION

To start an Xterm session, click on the UNIX Terminal icon on your desktop, or from the drop-down menus

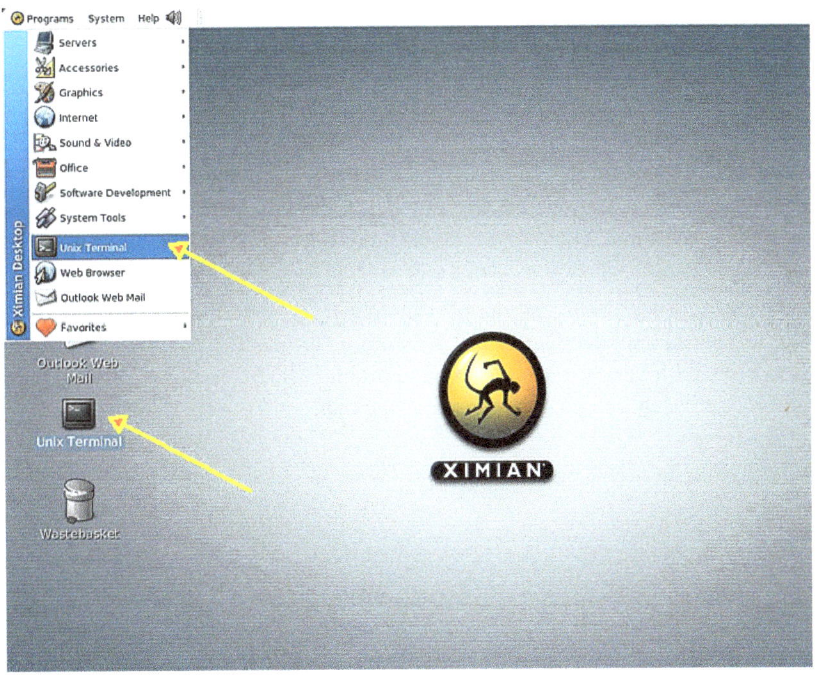

An Xterminal window will appear with a UNIX prompt, waiting for you to start entering commands.

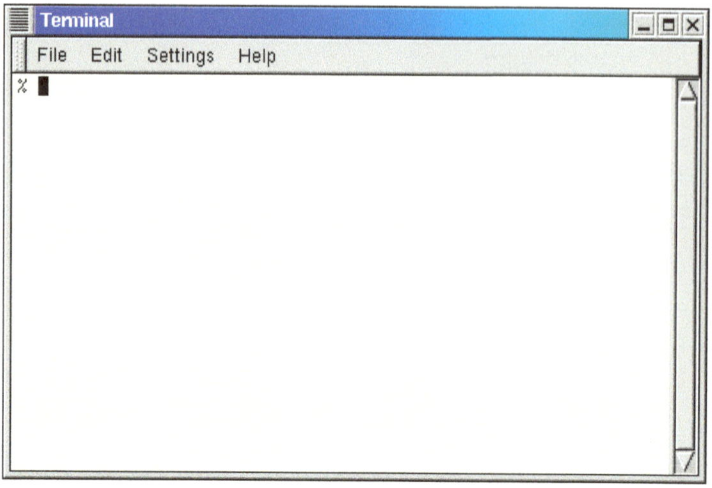

Listing files and directories

ls (list)

When you first login, your current working directory is your home directory. Your home directory has the same name as your user-name, for example, ee91ab, and it is where your personal files and subdirectories are saved.

To find out what is in your home directory, type

% ls (short for list)

The ls command lists the contents of your current working directory.

There may be no files visible in your home directory, in which case, the UNIX prompt will be returned. Alternatively, there may already be some files inserted by the System Administrator when your account was created.

ls does not, in fact, cause all the files in your home directory to be listed, but only those ones whose name does not begin with a dot (.) Files beginning with a dot (.) are known as hidden files and usually contain important program configuration information. They are hidden because you should not change them unless you are very familiar with UNIX!!!

To list all files in your home directory including those whose names begin with a dot, type

% ls -a

ls is an example of a command which can take options: -a is an example of an option. The options change the behaviour of the command. There are online manual pages that tell you which options a particular command can take, and how each option modifies the behaviour of the command. (See later in this tutorial)

Making Directories

mkdir (make directory)

We will now make a subdirectory in your home directory to hold the files you will be creating and using in the course of this tutorial. To make a subdirectory called unixstuff in your current working directory type

% mkdir unixstuff

To see the directory you have just created, type

% ls

Changing to a different directory

cd (change directory)

The command cd *directory* means change the current working directory to 'directory'. The current working directory may be thought of as the directory you are in, i.e. your current position in the file-system tree.

To change to the directory you have just made, type

% cd unixstuff

Type ls to see the contents (which should be empty)

Exercise 1a

Make another directory inside the **unixstuff** directory called **backups**

The directories . and ..

Still in the **unixstuff** directory, type

% ls -a

As you can see, in the **unixstuff** directory (and in all other directories), there are two special directories called (.) and (..)

In UNIX, (.) means the current directory, so typing

% cd .

NOTE: there is a space between cd and the dot

means stay where you are (the **unixstuff** directory).

This may not seem very useful at first, but using (.) as the name of the current directory will save a lot of typing, as we shall see later in the tutorial.

(..) means the parent of the current directory, so typing

% cd ..

will take you one directory up the hierarchy (back to your home directory). Try it now.

Note: typing cd with no argument always returns you to your home directory. This is very useful if you are lost in the file system.

Pathnames

pwd (print working directory)

Pathnames enable you to work out where you are in relation to the whole file-system. For example, to find out the absolute pathname of your home-directory, type cd to get back to your home-directory and then type

% pwd

The full pathname will look something like this -

/a/fservb/fservb/fservb22/eebeng99/ee91ab

which means that ee91ab (your home directory) is in the directory eebeng99 (the group directory),which is located on the fservb file-server.

Note:

/a/fservb/fservb/fservb22/eebeng99/ee91ab

can be shortened to

/user/eebeng99/ee91ab

Exercise 1b

Use the commands ls, pwd and cd to explore the file system.

(Remember, if you get lost, type cd by itself to return to your home-directory)

More about home directories and pathnames

Understanding pathnames

First type cd to get back to your home-directory, then type

% ls unixstuff

to list the conents of your unixstuff directory.

Now type

% ls backups

You will get a message like this -

backups: No such file or directory

The reason is, **backups** is not in your current working directory. To use a command on a file (or directory) not in the current working directory (the directory you are currently in), you must either cd to the correct directory, or specify its full pathname. To list the contents of your backups directory, you must type

% ls unixstuff/backups

~ (your home directory)

Home directories can also be referred to by the tilde ~ character. It can be used to specify paths starting at your home directory. So typing

% ls ~/unixstuff

will list the contents of your unixstuff directory, no matter where you currently are in the file system.

What do you think

% ls ~

would list?

What do you think

% ls ~/..

would list?

Summary

ls	list files and directories
ls -a	list all files and directories
mkdir	make a directory
cd *directory*	change to named directory
cd	change to home-directory
cd ~	change to home-directory
cd ..	change to parent directory
pwd	display the path of the current directory

Copying Files

cp (copy)

cp *file1 file2* is the command which makes a copy of **file1** in the current working directory and calls it **file2**

What we are going to do now, is to take a file stored in an open access area of the file system, and use the cp command to copy it to your unixstuff directory.

First, cd to your unixstuff directory.

% cd ~/unixstuff

Then at the UNIX prompt, type,

% cp /vol/examples/tutorial/science.txt .

(Note: Don›t forget the dot (.) at the end. Remember, in UNIX, the dot means the current directory.)

The above command means copy the file **science.txt** to the current directory, keeping the name the same.

(Note: The directory **/vol/examples/tutorial/** is an area to which everyone in the department has read and copy access. If you are from outside the University, you can grab a copy of the file here. Use ‹File/Save As..› from the menu bar to save it into your **unixstuff** directory.)

Exercise 2a

Create a backup of your **science.txt** file by copying it to a file called **science.bak**

Moving files

mv (move)

mv *file1 file2* moves (or renames) **file1** to **file2**

To move a file from one place to another, use the mv command. This has the effect of moving rather than copying the file, so you end up with only one file rather than two.

It can also be used to rename a file, by moving the file to the same directory, but giving it a different name.

We are now going to move the file science.bak to your backup directory.

First, change directories to your unixstuff directory (can you remember how?). Then, inside the **unixstuff** directory, type

% mv science.bak backups/.

Type ls and ls backups to see if it has worked.

Removing files and directories

rm (remove), rmdir (remove directory)

To delete (remove) a file, use the rm command. As an example, we are going to create a copy of the **science.txt** file then delete it.

Inside your **unixstuff** directory, type

% cp science.txt tempfile.txt

% ls (to check if it has created the file)

% rm tempfile.txt

% ls (to check if it has deleted the file)

You can use the rmdir command to remove a directory (make sure it is empty first). Try to remove the **backups** directory. You will not be able to since UNIX will not let you remove a non-empty directory.

Exercise 2b

Create a directory called **tempstuff** using mkdir , then remove it using the rmdir command.

Displaying the contents of a file on the screen

clear (clear screen)

Before you start the next section, you may like to clear the terminal window of the previous commands so the output of the following commands can be clearly understood.

At the prompt, type

% clear

This will clear all text and leave you with the % prompt at the top of the window.

cat (concatenate)

The command cat can be used to display the contents of a file on the screen. Type:

% cat science.txt

As you can see, the file is longer than than the size of the window, so it scrolls past making it unreadable.

less

The command less writes the contents of a file onto the screen a page at a time. Type

% less science.txt

Press the [space-bar] if you want to see another page, type [q] if you want to quit reading. As you can see, less is used in preference to cat for long files.

head

The head command writes the first ten lines of a file to the screen.

First clear the screen then type

% head science.txt

Then type

% head -5 science.txt

What difference did the -5 do to the head command?

tail

The tail command writes the last ten lines of a file to the screen.

Clear the screen and type

% tail science.txt

How can you view the last 15 lines of the file?

Searching the contents of a file

Simple searching using less

Using less, you can search though a text file for a keyword (pattern). For example, to search through **science.txt** for the word 'science', type

% less science.txt

then, still in less (i.e. don›t press [q] to quit), type a forward slash [/] followed by the word to search

/science

As you can see, less finds and highlights the keyword. Type [n] to search for the next occurrence of the word.

grep (don't ask why it is called grep)

grep is one of many standard UNIX utilities. It searches files for specified words or patterns. First clear the screen, then type

% grep science science.txt

As you can see, grep has printed out each line containg the word science.

Or has it????

Try typing

% grep Science science.txt

The grep command is case sensitive; it distinguishes between Science and science.

To ignore upper/lower case distinctions, use the -i option, i.e. type

% grep -i science science.txt

To search for a phrase or pattern, you must enclose it in single quotes (the apostrophe symbol). For example to search for spinning top, type

% grep -i ‹spinning top› science.txt

Some of the other options of grep are:

-v display those lines that do NOT match

-n precede each matching line with the line number

-c print only the total count of matched lines

Try some of them and see the different results. Don›t forget, you can use more than one option at a time, for example, the number of lines without the words science or Science is

% grep -ivc science science.txt

wc (word count)

A handy little utility is the wc command, short for word count. To do a word count on **science.txt**, type

% wc -w science.txt

To find out how many lines the file has, type

% wc -l science.txt

Summary

cp *file1 file2*	copy file1 and call it file2
mv *file1 file2*	move or rename file1 to file2
rm *file*	remove a file
rmdir *directory*	remove a directory
cat *file*	display a file
more *file*	display a file a page at a time
head *file*	display the first few lines of a file
tail *file*	display the last few lines of a file
grep *'keyword' file*	search a file for keywords
wc *file*	count number of lines/words/characters in file

Redirection

Most processes initiated by UNIX commands write to the standard output (that is, they write to the terminal screen), and many take their input from the standard input (that is, they read it from the keyboard). There is also the standard error, where processes write their error messages, by default, to the terminal screen.

We have already seen one use of the cat command to write the contents of a file to the screen.

Now type cat without specifing a file to read

% cat

Then type a few words on the keyboard and press the [Return] key.

Finally hold the [Ctrl] key down and press [d] (written as ^D for short) to end the input.

What has happened?

If you run the cat command without specifing a file to read, it reads the standard input (the keyboard), and on receiving the'end of file' (^D), copies it to the standard output (the screen).

In UNIX, we can redirect both the input and the output of commands.

Redirecting the Output

We use the > symbol to redirect the output of a command. For example, to create a file called **list1** containing a list of fruit, type

% cat > list1

Then type in the names of some fruit. Press [Return] after each one.

Pear

Banana

Apple

^D (Control D to stop)

What happens is the cat command reads the standard input (the keyboard) and the > redirects the output, which normally goes to the screen, into a file called **list1**

To read the contents of the file, type

% cat list1

Exercise 3a

Using the above method, create another file called **list2** containing the following fruit: orange, plum, mango, grapefruit. Read the contents of **list2**

The form >> appends standard output to a file. So to add more items to the file **list1**, type

% cat >> list1

Then type in the names of more fruit

Peach

Grape

Orange

^D (Control D to stop)

To read the contents of the file, type

% cat list1

You should now have two files. One contains six fruit, the other contains four fruit. We will now use the cat command to join (concatenate) **list1** and **list2**into a new file called **biglist**. Type

% cat list1 list2 > biglist

What this is doing is reading the contents of **list1** and **list2** in turn, then outputing the text to the file **biglist**

To read the contents of the new file, type

% cat biglist

Redirecting the Input

We use the < symbol to redirect the input of a command.

The command sort alphabetically or numerically sorts a list. Type

% sort

Then type in the names of some vegetables. Press [Return] after each one.

Carrot

Beetroot

Artichoke

^D (control d to stop)

The output will be

Artichoke

beetroot

carrot

Using < you can redirect the input to come from a file rather than the keyboard. For example, to sort the list of fruit, type

% sort < biglist

and the sorted list will be output to the screen.

To output the sorted list to a file, type,

% sort < biglist > slist

Use cat to read the contents of the file **slist**

Pipes

To see who is on the system with you, type

% who

One method to get a sorted list of names is to type,

% who > names.txt

% sort < names.txt

This is a bit slow and you have to remember to remove the temporary file called names when you have finished. What you really want to do is connect the output of the who command directly to the input of the sort command. This is exactly what pipes do. The symbol for a pipe is the vertical bar |

For example, typing

% who | sort

will give the same result as above, but quicker and cleaner.

To find out how many users are logged on, type

% who | wc -l

Exercise 3b

a2ps -Phockney *textfile* is the command to print a postscript file to the printer hockney.

Using pipes, print all lines of **list1** and **list2** containing the letter 'p', sort the result, and print to the printer hockney.

Summary

command > *file*	redirect standard output to a file
command >> *file*	append standard output to a file
command < *file*	redirect standard input from a file
command1 | *command2*	pipe the output of command1 to the input of command2
cat *file1 file2* > *file0*	concatenate file1 and file2 to file0
sort	sort data
who	list users currently logged in
a2ps -P*printer textfile*	print text file to named printer
lpr -P*printer psfile*	print postscript file to named printer

Wildcards

The characters * and ?

The character * is called a wildcard, and will match against none or more character(s) in a file (or directory) name. For example, in your **unixstuff**directory, type

% ls list*

This will list all files in the current directory starting with **list....**

Try typing

% ls *list

This will list all files in the current directory ending with **....list**

The character ? will match exactly one character.

So ls ?ouse will match files like **house** and **mouse**, but not **grouse**.

Try typing

% ls ?list

Filename conventions

We should note here that a directory is merely a special type of file. So the rules and conventions for naming files apply also to directories.

In naming files, characters with special meanings such as / * **& %** , should be avoided. Also, avoid using spaces within names. The safest way to name a file is to use only alphanumeric characters, that is, letters and numbers, together with _ (underscore) and . (dot).

File names conventionally start with a lower-case letter, and may end with a dot followed by a group of letters indicating the contents of the file. For example, all files consisting of C code may be named with the ending .c, for example, prog1.c . Then in order to list all files containing C code in your home directory, you need only type ls *.c in that directory.

Beware: some applications give the same name to all the output files they generate.

For example, some compilers, unless given the appropriate option, produce compiled files named **a.out**. Should you forget to use that option, you are advised to rename the compiled file immediately, otherwise the next such file will overwrite it and it will be lost.

Getting Help

On-line Manuals

There are on-line manuals which gives information about most commands. The manual pages tell you which options a particular command can take, and how each option modifies the behaviour of the command. Type man command to read the manual page for a particular command.

For example, to find out more about the wc (word count) command, type

% man wc

Alternatively

% whatis wc

gives a one-line description of the command, but omits any information about options etc.

Apropos

When you are not sure of the exact name of a command,

% apropos keyword

will give you the commands with keyword in their manual page header. For example, try typing

% apropos copy

Summary

*	match any number of characters
?	match one character
man *command*	read the online manual page for a command
whatis *command*	brief description of a command
apropos *keyword*	match commands with keyword in their man pages

File system security (access rights)

In your unixstuff directory, type

% ls -l (l for long listing!)

You will see that you now get lots of details about the contents of your directory, similar to the example below.

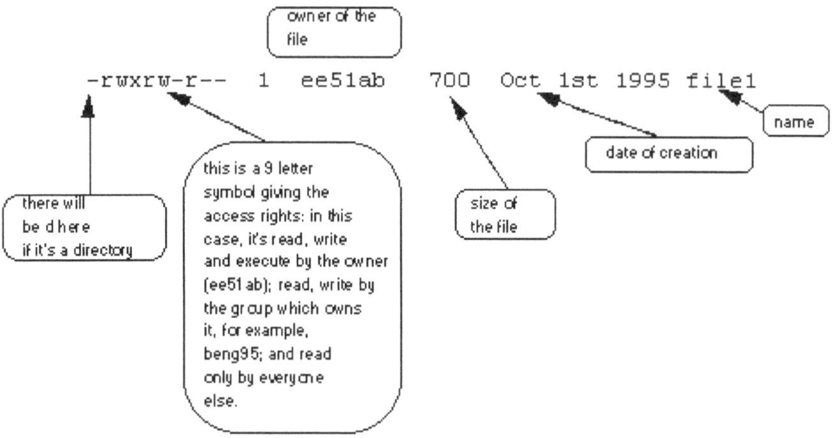

Each file (and directory) has associated access rights, which may be found by typing ls -l. Also, ls -lg gives additional information as to which group owns the file (beng95 in the following example):

-rwxrw-r-- 1 ee51ab beng95 2450 Sept29 11:52 file1

In the left-hand column is a 10 symbol string consisting of the symbols d, r, w, x, -, and, occasionally, s or S. If d is present, it will be at the left hand end of the string, and indicates a directory: otherwise - will be the starting symbol of the string.

The 9 remaining symbols indicate the permissions, or access rights, and are taken as three groups of 3.

- The left group of 3 gives the file permissions for the user that owns the file (or directory) (ee51ab in the above example);
- the middle group gives the permissions for the group of people to whom the file (or directory) belongs (eebeng95 in the above example);

- the rightmost group gives the permissions for all others.

The symbols r, w, etc., have slightly different meanings depending on whether they refer to a simple file or to a directory.

Access rights on files.

- r (or -), indicates read permission (or otherwise), that is, the presence or absence of permission to read and copy the file
- w (or -), indicates write permission (or otherwise), that is, the permission (or otherwise) to change a file
- x (or -), indicates execution permission (or otherwise), that is, the permission to execute a file, where appropriate

Access rights on directories.

- r allows users to list files in the directory;
- w means that users may delete files from the directory or move files into it;
- x means the right to access files in the directory. This implies that you may read files in the directory provided you have read permission on the individual files.

So, in order to read a file, you must have execute permission on the directory containing that file, and hence on any directory containing that directory as a subdirectory, and so on, up the tree.

Some examples

-rwxrwxrwx	a file that everyone can read, write and execute (and delete).
-rw-------	a file that only the owner can read and write - no-one else can read or write and no-one has execution rights (e.g. your mailbox file).

Changing access rights

chmod (changing a file mode)

Only the owner of a file can use chmod to change the permissions of a file. The options of chmod are as follows

Symbol	Meaning
u	user
g	group
o	other
a	all
r	read

w	write (and delete)
x	execute (and access directory)
+	add permission
-	take away permission

For example, to remove read write and execute permissions on the file biglist for the group and others, type

% chmod go-rwx biglist

This will leave the other permissions unaffected.

To give read and write permissions on the file **biglist** to all,

% chmod a+rw biglist

Exercise 5a

Try changing access permissions on the file **science.txt** and on the directory **backups**

Use ls -l to check that the permissions have changed.

Processes and Jobs

A process is an executing program identified by a unique PID (process identifier). To see information about your processes, with their associated PID and status, type

% ps

A process may be in the foreground, in the background, or be suspended. In general the shell does not return the UNIX prompt until the current process has finished executing.

Some processes take a long time to run and hold up the terminal. Backgrounding a long process has the effect that the UNIX prompt is returned immediately, and other tasks can be carried out while the original process continues executing.

Running background processes

To background a process, type an **&** at the end of the command line. For example, the command sleep waits a given number of seconds before continuing. Type

% sleep 10

This will wait 10 seconds before returning the command prompt %. Until the command prompt is returned, you can do nothing except wait.

To run sleep in the background, type

% sleep 10 &

[1] 6259

The **&** runs the job in the background and returns the prompt straight away, allowing you do run other programs while waiting for that one to finish.

The first line in the above example is typed in by the user; the next line, indicating job number and PID, is returned by the machine. The user is be notified of a job number (numbered from 1) enclosed in square brackets, together with a PID and is notified when a background process is finished. Backgrounding is useful for jobs which will take a long time to complete.

Backgrounding a current foreground process

At the prompt, type

% sleep 100

You can suspend the process running in the foreground by holding down the [control] key and typing [z] (written as ^**Z**) Then to put it in the background, type

% bg

Note: do not background programs that require user interaction e.g. pine

Listing suspended and background processes

When a process is running, backgrounded or suspended, it will be entered onto a list along with a job number. To examine this list, type

% jobs

An example of a job list could be

[1] Suspended sleep 100

[2] Running netscape

[3] Running nedit

To restart (foreground) a suspended processes, type

% fg %jobnumber

For example, to restart sleep 100, type

% fg %1

Typing fg with no job number foregrounds the last suspended process.

Killing a process

kill (terminate or signal a process)

It is sometimes necessary to kill a process (for example, when an executing program is in an infinite loop)

To kill a job running in the foreground, type ^C (control c). For example, run

% sleep 100

^C

To kill a suspended or background process, type

% kill %jobnumber

For example, run

% sleep 100 &

% jobs

If it is job number 4, type

% kill %4

To check whether this has worked, examine the job list again to see if the process has been removed.

ps (process status)

Alternatively, processes can be killed by finding their process numbers (PIDs) and using kill *PID_number*

% sleep 100 &

% ps

PID TT S TIME COMMAND

20077 pts/5 S 0:05 sleep 100

21563 pts/5 T 0:00 netscape

21873 pts/5 S 0:25 nedit

To kill off the process sleep 100, type

% kill 20077

and then type ps again to see if it has been removed from the list.

If a process refuses to be killed, uses the **-9** option, i.e. type

% kill -9 20077

Note: It is not possible to kill off other users› processes !!!

Summary

ls -lag	list access rights for all files
chmod [*options*] *file*	change access rights for named file
command &	run command in background
^C	kill the job running in the foreground
^Z	suspend the job running in the foreground
bg	background the suspended job
jobs	list current jobs
fg %1	foreground job number 1
kill %1	kill job number 1

ps	list current processes
kill 26152	kill process number 26152

Other useful UNIX commands

quota

All students are allocated a certain amount of disk space on the file system for their personal files, usually about 100Mb. If you go over your quota, you are given 7 days to remove excess files.

To check your current quota and how much of it you have used, type

% quota –v

df

The df command reports on the space left on the file system. For example, to find out how much space is left on the fileserver, type

% df .

du

The du command outputs the number of kilobyes used by each subdirectory. Useful if you have gone over quota and you want to find out which directory has the most files. In your home-directory, type

% du

compress

This reduces the size of a file, thus freeing valuable disk space. For example, type

% ls -l science.txt

and note the size of the file. Then to compress science.txt, type

% compress science.txt

This will compress the file and place it in a file called science.txt.Z

To see the change in size, type ls -l again.

To uncomress the file, use the uncompress command.

% uncompress science.txt.Z

gzip

This also compresses a file, and is more efficient than compress. For example, to zip science.txt, type

% gzip science.txt

This will zip the file and place it in a file called science.txt.gz

To unzip the file, use the gunzip command.

% gunzip science.txt.gz

file

file classifies the named files according to the type of data they contain, for example ascii (text), pictures, compressed data, etc.. To report on all files in your home directory, type

% file *

history

The C shell keeps an ordered list of all the commands that you have entered. Each command is given a number according to the order it was entered.

% history (show command history list)

If you are using the C shell, you can use the exclamation character (!) to recall commands easily.

% !! (recall last command)

% !-3 (recall third most recent command)

% !5 (recall 5th command in list)

% !grep (recall last command starting with grep)

You can increase the size of the history buffer by typing

% set history=100

Compiling UNIX software packages

We have many public domain and commercial software packages installed on our systems, which are available to all users. However, students are allowed to download and install small software packages in their own home directory, software usually only useful to them personally.

There are a number of steps needed to install the software.

- Locate and download the source code (which is usually compressed)
- Unpack the source code
- Compile the code
- Install the resulting executable
- Set paths to the installation directory

Of the above steps, probably the most difficult is the compilation stage.

Compiling Source Code

All high-level language code must be converted into a form the computer understands. For example, C language source code is converted into a lower-level language called assembly language. The assembly language code made by the previous stage is then converted into object code which are fragments of code which the computer understands directly. The final stage in compiling a program involves linking the object code to code libraries which contain certain built-in functions. This final stage produces an executable program.

To do all these steps by hand is complicated and beyond the capability of the ordinary user. A number of utilities and tools have been developed for programmers and end-users to simplify these steps.

make and the Makefile

The make command allows programmers to manage large programs or groups of programs. It aids in developing large programs by keeping track of which portions of the entire program have been changed, compiling only those parts of the program which have changed since the last compile.

The make program gets its set of compile rules from a text file called **Makefile** which resides in the same directory as the source files. It contains information on how to compile the software, e.g. the optimisation level, whether to include debugging info in the executable. It also contains information on where to install the finished compiled binaries (executables), manual pages, data files, dependent library files, configuration files, etc.

Some packages require you to edit the Makefile by hand to set the final installation directory and any other parameters. However, many packages are now being distributed with the GNU configure utility.

configure

As the number of UNIX variants increased, it became harder to write programs which could run on all variants. Developers frequently did not have access to every system, and the characteristics of some systems changed from version to version. The GNU configure and build system simplifies the building of programs distributed as source code. All programs are built using a simple, standardised, two step process. The program builder need not install any special tools in order to build the program.

The configure shell script attempts to guess correct values for various system-dependent variables used during compilation. It uses those values to create a **Makefile** in each directory of the package.

The simplest way to compile a package is:

- cd to the directory containing the package's source code.
- Type ./configure to configure the package for your system.
- Type make to compile the package.

- Optionally, type make check to run any self-tests that come with the package.
- Type make install to install the programs and any data files and documentation.
- Optionally, type make clean to remove the program binaries and object files from the source code directory

The configure utility supports a wide variety of options. You can usually use the --help option to get a list of interesting options for a particular configure script.

The only generic options you are likely to use are the --prefix and --exec-prefix options. These options are used to specify the installation directories.

The directory named by the --prefix option will hold machine independent files such as documentation, data and configuration files.

The directory named by the --exec-prefix option, (which is normally a subdirectory of the --prefix directory), will hold machine dependent files such as executables.

Downloading source code

For this example, we will download a piece of free software that converts between different units of measurements.

First create a download directory

% mkdir download

Extracting the source code

Go into your **download** directory and list the contents.

% cd download

% ls -l

As you can see, the filename ends in tar.gz. The tar command turns several files and directories into one single tar file. This is then compressed using the gzip command (to create a tar.gz file).

First unzip the file using the gunzip command. This will create a .tar file.

% gunzip units-1.74.tar.gz

Then extract the contents of the tar file.

% tar -xvf units-1.74.tar

Again, list the contents of the **download** directory, then go to the **units-1.74** sub-directory.

% cd units-1.74

Configuring and creating the Makefile

The first thing to do is carefully read the **README** and **INSTALL** text files (use the less command). These contain important information on how to compile and run the software.

The units package uses the GNU configure system to compile the source code. We will need to specify the installation directory, since the default will be the main system area which you will not have write permissions for. We need to create an install directory in your home directory.

% mkdir ~/units174

Then run the configure utility setting the installation path to this.

% ./configure --prefix=$HOME/units174

NOTE:

The **$HOME** variable is an example of an environment variable.

The value of **$HOME** is the path to your home directory. Just type

% echo $HOME

to show the contents of this variable. We will learn more about environment variables in a later chapter.

If configure has run correctly, it will have created a Makefile with all necessary options. You can view the Makefile if you wish (use the less command), but do not edit the contents of this.

Building the package

Now you can go ahead and build the package by running the make command.

% make

After a minute or two (depending on the speed of the computer), the executables will be created. You can check to see everything compiled successfully by typing

% make check

If everything is okay, you can now install the package.

% make install

This will install the files into the **~/units174** directory you created earlier.

Running the software

You are now ready to run the software (assuming everything worked).

% cd ~/units174

If you list the contents of the units directory, you will see a number of subdirectories.

bin	The binary executables
info	GNU info formatted documentation
man	Man pages
share	Shared data files

To run the program, change to the **bin** directory and type

% ./units

As an example, convert 6 feet to metres.

You have: 6 feet

You want: metres

* 1.8288

If you get the answer 1.8288, congratulations, it worked.

To view what units it can convert between, view the data file in the share directory (the list is quite comprehensive).

To read the full documentation, change into the **info** directory and type

% info --file=units.info

Stripping unnecessary code

When a piece of software is being developed, it is useful for the programmer to include debugging information into the resulting executable. This way, if there are problems encountered when running the executable, the programmer can load the executable into a debugging software package and track down any software bugs.

This is useful for the programmer, but unnecessary for the user. We can assume that the package, once finished and available for download has already been tested and debugged. However, when we compiled the software above, debugging information was still compiled into the final executable. Since it is unlikey that we are going to need this debugging information, we can strip it out of the final executable. One of the advantages of this is a much smaller executable, which should run slightly faster.

What we are going to do is look at the before and after size of the binary file. First change into the **bin** directory of the units installation directory.

% cd ~/units174/bin

% ls -l

As you can see, the file is over 100 kbytes in size. You can get more information on the type of file by using the file command.

% file units

units: ELF 32-bit LSB executable, Intel 80386, version 1, dynamically linked (uses shared libs), not stripped

To strip all the debug and line numbering information out of the binary file, use the strip command

% strip units

% ls -l

As you can see, the file is now 36 kbytes - a third of its original size. Two thirds of the binary file was debug code !!!

Check the file information again.

% file units

units: ELF 32-bit LSB executable, Intel 80386, version 1, dynamically linked (uses shared libs), stripped

HINT: You can use the make command to install pre-stripped copies of all the binary files when you install the package.

Instead of typing make install, simply type make install-strip

UNIX Variables

Variables are a way of passing information from the shell to programs when you run them. Programs look "in the environment" for particular variables and if they are found will use the values stored. Some are set by the system, others by you, yet others by the shell, or any program that loads another program.

Standard UNIX variables are split into two categories, environment variables and shell variables. In broad terms, shell variables apply only to the current instance of the shell and are used to set short-term working conditions; environment variables have a farther reaching significance, and those set at login are valid for the duration of the session. By convention, environment variables have UPPER CASE and shell variables have lower case names.

Environment Variables

An example of an environment variable is the OSTYPE variable. The value of this is the current operating system you are using. Type

% echo $OSTYPE

More examples of environment variables are

- USER (your login name)
- HOME (the path name of your home directory)
- HOST (the name of the computer you are using)
- ARCH (the architecture of the computers processor)
- DISPLAY (the name of the computer screen to display X windows)
- PRINTER (the default printer to send print jobs)
- PATH (the directories the shell should search to find a command)

Finding out the current values of these variables.

ENVIRONMENT variables are set using the setenv command, displayed using the printenv or env commands, and unset using the unsetenvcommand.

To show all values of these variables, type

% printenv | less

Shell Variables

An example of a shell variable is the history variable. The value of this is how many shell commands to save, allow the user to scroll back through all the commands they have previously entered. Type

% echo $history

More examples of shell variables are

- cwd (your current working directory)
- home (the path name of your home directory)
- path (the directories the shell should search to find a command)
- prompt (the text string used to prompt for interactive commands shell your login shell)

Finding out the current values of these variables.

SHELL variables are both set and displayed using the set command. They can be unset by using the unset command.

To show all values of these variables, type

% set | less

So what is the difference between PATH and path ?

In general, environment and shell variables that have the same name (apart from the case) are distinct and independent, except for possibly having the same initial values. There are, however, exceptions.

Each time the shell variables home, user and term are changed, the corresponding environment variables HOME, USER and TERM receive the same values. However, altering the environment variables has no effect on the corresponding shell variables.

PATH and path specify directories to search for commands and programs. Both variables always represent the same directory list, and altering either automatically causes the other to be changed.

Using and setting variables

Each time you login to a UNIX host, the system looks in your home directory for initialisation files. Information in these files is used to set up your working environment. The C and TC shells uses two files called .login and .cshrc (note that both file names begin with a dot).

At login the C shell first reads **.cshrc** followed by **.login**

.login is to set conditions which will apply to the whole session and to perform actions that are relevant only at login.

.cshrc is used to set conditions and perform actions specific to the shell and to each invocation of it.

The guidelines are to set ENVIRONMENT variables in the **.login** file and SHELL variables in the **.cshrc** file.

WARNING: NEVER put commands that run graphical displays (e.g. a web browser) in your .cshrc or .login file.

Setting shell variables in the .cshrc file

For example, to change the number of shell commands saved in the history list, you need to set the shell variable history. It is set to 100 by default, but you can increase this if you wish.

% set history = 200

Check this has worked by typing

% echo $history

However, this has only set the variable for the lifetime of the current shell. If you open a new xterm window, it will only have the default history value set. To PERMANENTLY set the value of history, you will need to add the set command to the .cshrc file.

First open the **.cshrc** file in a text editor. An easy, user-friendly editor to use is nedit.

% nedit ~/.cshrc

Add the following line AFTER the list of other commands.

set history = 200

Save the file and force the shell to reread its .cshrc file buy using the shell source command.

% source .cshrc

Check this has worked by typing

% echo $history

Setting the path

When you type a command, your path (or PATH) variable defines in which directories the shell will look to find the command you typed. If the system returns a message saying "command: Command not found", this indicates that either the command doesn't exist at all on the system or it is simply not in your path.

For example, to run units, you either need to directly specify the units path, or you need to have the directory in your path.

You can add it to the end of your existing path (the **$path** represents this) by issuing the command:

% set path = ($path ~/units174/bin)

Test that this worked by trying to run units in any directory other that where units is actually located.

% cd; units

HINT: You can run multiple commands on one line by separating them with a semicolon.

To add this path PERMANENTLY, add the following line to your .cshrc AFTER the list of other commands.

set path = ($path ~/units174/bin)

SECTION II: BASIC PROGRAMMING TECHNIQUES

2

CHAPTER

BASIC PROGRAMMING TECHNIQUES

Mark Burgess

WHAT IS UNIX PROGRAMMING?

UNIX is one of the most important operating system in use today, perhaps even *the* most important. Since its invention around the beginning of the 1970s it has been an object of continual research and development. UNIX is not popular because it is the best operating system one could imagine, but because it is an extremely flexible system which is easy to extend and modify. It is an ideal platform for developing new ideas.

Much of the success of UNIX may be attributed to the rapid pace of its development (a development to which all of its users have been able to contribute) its efficiency at running programs and the many powerful tools which have been written for it over the years, such as the C programming language, make, shell, lex and yacc and many others. UNIX was written by programmers for programmers. It is popular in situations where a lot of computing power is required and for database applications, where timesharing is critical. In contrast to some operating systems, UNIX performs equally well on large scale computers (with many processors) and small computers which fit in your suitcase!

All of the basic mechanisms required of a multi-user operating system are present in UNIX. During the last few years it has become ever more popular and has formed the basis of newer, though less mature, systems like NT. One reason for this that now computers have now become powerful enough to run UNIX effectively. UNIX places burdens on the resources of a computer, since it expects to be able to run potentially many programs simultaneously.

If you are coming to UNIX from Windows or DOS you may well be used to using applications software or helpful interactive utilities to solve every problem. UNIX is not usually like this: the operating system has much greater functionality and provides

Citation: Mark Burgess, Basic Programming techniques, http://www.iu.hio.no/~mark/unix/unix.html.

the possibilities for making your own, so it is less common to find applications software which implements the same things. In UNIX you are usually asked to learn a language in order to express exactly what you want. This is much more powerful than menu systems, but it is harder to learn

UNIX has long been in the hands of academics who are used to making their own applications or writing their own programs, whereas as the Windows world has been driven by businesses who are willing to spend money on software. For that reason commercial UNIX software is often very expensive and therefore not available at this college. On the other hand, the flexibility of UNIX means that it is easy to write programs and it is possible to fetch gigabytes of *free software* from the Internet to suit your needs. It may not look exactly like what you are used to on your PC, but then you have to remember that UNIX users are a different kind of animal altogether

Like all operating systems, UNIX has many faults. The biggest problem for any operating system is that it evolves without being redesigned. Operating systems evolve as more and more patches and hacks are applied to solve day-to-day problems. The result is either a mess which works somehow (like UNIX) or a blank refusal to change (like DOS or the MacIntosh, prior to MacOS X, which is based on BSD UNIX). From a practical perspective, UNIX is important and successful because it is a multi-process system which

- has an enormous functionality built in, and the capacity to adapt itself to changing technologies,
- is relatively portable,
- is good at sharing resources (but not so good at security),
- has tools which are each developed to do *one thing well,*
- allows these tools to be combined in every imaginable way, using pipes and channeling of data streams,
- incorporates networking almost trivially, because all the right mechanisms are already there for providing services and sharing, building client-server pairs etc,.
- it is very adaptable and is often used to develop new ideas because of the rich variety of tools it possesses.

UNIX has some problems: it is old, it contains a lot of rubbish which no one ever bothered to throw away. Although it develops quickly (at light speed compared to either DOS/Windows or MacIntosh) the user interface has been the slowest thing to change. UNIX is not user-friendly for beginners, it is user-friendly for advanced users: it is made for users who *know* about computing. It sometimes makes simple things difficult, but above all it makes things possible!

The aim of this introduction is to

- introduce the UNIX system basics and user interface,
- develop the UNIX philosophy of using and combining tools,
- learn how to make new tools and write software,
- learn how to understand existing software.

To accomplish this task, we must first learn something about the shell language (the way in which UNIX starts programs). Later we shall learn how to solve more complex problems using Perl and C. Each of these is a language which can be used to put UNIX to work. We must also learn when to use which tool, so that we do not waste time and effort. Typical uses for these different interfaces are

shell

Command line interaction, making scripts which performs simple jobs such as running programs, installing new software, simple system configuration and administration.

perl

Text interpretation, text formatting, output filters, mail robots, WWW cgi (common gateway interface) scripts in forms, password testing, simple database manipulation, simple client-server applications.

C

Nearly all of UNIX is written in C. Any program which cannot be solved quickly using shell or perl can be written in C. One advantage is that C is a compiled language and many simple errors can be caught at compile time.

Much of UNIX's recent popularity has been a result of its networking abilities: UNIX is the backbone of the Internet. No other widely available system could keep the Internet alive today. GNU/Linux is a free/open source re-write of the UNIX operating system, which many enhancements. While GNU/Linux is not "rocket science" to computer experts, it has distilled the essence of UNIX and placed it in the hands of everyone. It runs on wrist watches and mainframe computers. Like it or loathe it, GNU/Linux is probably the most important single development in computer operating systems for many years.

Once you have mastered the UNIX interface and philosophy you will find that i) the PC and MacIntosh window environments might seem to be easy to use, but are simplistic and primitive by comparison; ii) UNIX is far from being the perfect operating system--it has a whole different set of problems and flaws.

The operating system of the future will not be UNIX or GNU/Linux as we see it today (hopefully), nor will is be DOS or MacIntosh, but one thing is for certain: it will owe a lot to the UNIX operating system and will contain many of the tools and mechanisms we shall describe below.

FLAVOURS OF UNIX

UNIX is not a single operating system. It has branched out in many different directions since it was introduced by AT&T. The most important `fork()' in its history happened early on when the university of Berkeley, California created the BSD (Berkeley Software Distribution), adding network support and the C-shell.

Here are some of the most common implementations of unix.

BSD:

Berkeley, BSD

SunOS:

Sun Microsystems, BSD/sys 5

Solaris:

Sun Microsystems, Sys 5/BSD

Ultrix:

Digital Equipment Corporation, BSD

OSF 1:

Digital Equipment Corporation, BSD/sys 5

HPUX:

Hewlett-Packard, Sys 5

AIX:

IBM, Sys 5 / BSD

IRIX:

Silicon Graphics, Sys 5

GNU/Linux:

GNU, BSD/Posix

How to use this reference guide

This programming guide is something between a user manual and a tutorial. The information contained here should be sufficient to get you started with the UNIX system, but it is far from complete.

To use this programming guide, you will need to work through the basics from each chapter. You will find that there is much more information here than you need straight away, so try not to be overwhelmed by the amount of material. Use the contents and the indices at the back to find the information you need. If you are following a one-semester UNIX course, you should probably concentrate on the following:

- The remainder of this introduction
- The detailed knowledge of the Bash shell
- A detailed knowledge of Perl, guided by chapter 6. This chapter provides pointers on how to get started in perl. It is not a substitute for the perl book.

- A sound appreciation of chapter 8 on network programming.

The *only* way to learn UNIX is to sit down and try it. As with any new thing, it is a pain to get started, but once you are started, you will probably come to agree that UNIX contains a wealth of possibilities, perhaps more than you had ever though was possible or useful!

One of the advantages of the UNIX system is that the entire UNIX manual is available on-line. You should get used to looking for information in the online manual pages. For instance, suppose you do not remember how to create a new directory, you could do the following:

```
nexus% man -k dir

dir        ls (1)        - list contents of directories
dirname    dirname (1)   - strip non-directory suffix from file name
dirs       bash (1)      - bash built-in commands, see bash(1)
find       find (1)      - search for files in a directory hierarchy
ls         ls (1)        - list contents of directories
mkdir      mkdir (1)     - make directories
pwd        pwd (1)       - print name of current/working directory
rmdir      rmdir (1)     - remove empty directories
```

The `man -k› command looks for a keyword in the manual and lists all the references it finds. The command `apropos› is completely equivalent to `man -k›. Having discovered that the command to create a directory is `mkdir› you can now look up the specific manual page on `mkdir› to find out how to use it:

```
man mkdir
```

Some but no all of the UNIX commands also have a help option which is activated with the `-h› or `--help› command-line option.

```
dax% mkdir --help
Usage: mkdir [OPTION] DIRECTORY...
  -p, --parents      no error if existing, make parent directories as needed
  -m, --mode=MODE    set permission mode (as in chmod), not 0777 - umask
      --help         display this help and exit
      --version      output version information and exit
dax%
```

NEVER- DO'S IN UNIX

There are some things that you should never do in UNIX. Some of these will cause you more serious problems than others. You can make your own list as you discover more.

- You should NEVER EVER switch off the power on a UNIX computer unless you know what you are doing. A UNIX machine is not like a PC running DOS. Even when you are not doing anything, the system is working in the background. If you switch off the power, you could interrupt the system while it is writing to the disk drive and destroy your disk. You must also remember that several users might be using the system even though you cannot see them: they do not have to be sitting at the machine, they could be logged in over the network. If you switch off the power, you might ruin their valuable work.
- Once you have deleted a UNIX file using rm it is impossible to recover it! Don't use wildcards with rm without thinking quite carefully about what you are doing! It has happened to very many users throughout the history of UNIX that one tries to type
- rm *~

but instead, by a slip of the hand, one writes

rm * ~

UNIX then takes these wildcards in turn, so that the first command is rm * which deletes all of your files! BE CAREFUL!

- Don't ever call a program or an important file `core'. Many scripts go around deleting files called `core' because the, when a program crashes, UNIX dumps the entire kernel image to a file called`core' and these files use up a lot of disk space. If you call a file `core' it might get deleted!
- Don't call test programs test. There is a UNIX command which is already called test and chances are that when you try to run your program you will start the UNIX command instead. This can cause a lot of confusion because the UNIX command doesn't seem to do very much at all!

What you should know before starting

One library: several interfaces

The core of UNIX is the library of functions (written in C) which access the system. Everything you do on a UNIX system goes through this set of functions. However, you can choose your own interface to these library functions. UNIX has very many different interfaces to its libraries in the form of languages and command interpreters.

You can use the functions directly in C, or you can use command programs like `ls', `cd' etc. These functions just provide a simple user interface to the C calls. You can also use a variety of `script' languages: C-shell, Bourne shell, Perl, Tcl, scheme. You choose the interface which solves your problem most easily.

UNIX commands are files

With the exception of a few simple commands which are built into the command interpreter (shell), all UNIX commands and programs consist of executable files.

In other words, there is a separate executable file for each command. This makes it extremely simple to add new commands to the system. One simply makes a program with the desired name and places it in the appropriate directory.

UNIX commands live in special directories (usually called bin for binary files). The location of these directories is recorded in a variable called path or PATH which is used by the system to search for binaries. We shall return to this in more detail in later chapters.

Kernel and Shell

Since users cannot command the kernel directly, UNIX has a command language known as the *shell*. The word shell implies a layer around the kernel. A shell is a user interface, or command interpreter.

There are two main versions of the shell, plus a number of enhancements.

/bin/sh

The Bourne Shell. The shell is most often used for writing system scripts. It is part of the original UNIX system.

/bin/csh

The C-shell. This was added to UNIX by the Berkeley workers. The commands and syntax resemble C code. C-shell is better suited for interactive work than the Bourne shell.

The program tcsh is a public-domain enhancement of the csh and is in common use. Two improved versions of the Bourne shell also exist: ksh, the Korn shell and bash, the Bourne-again shell.

Although the shells are mainly tools for typing in commands (which are executable files to be loaded and run), they contain features such as aliases, a command history, wildcard-expansions and job control functions which provide a comfortable user environment.

The role of C

Most of the UNIX kernel and daemons are written in the C programming language (1). Calls to the kernel and to services are made through functions in the standard C library. The commands like chmod, mkdirand cd are all C functions. The binary files of the same name /bin/chmod, /bin/mkdir etc. are just trivial "wrapper" programs for these C functions.

Until *Solaris 2*, the C compiler was a standard part of the UNIX operating system, thus C is the most natural language to program in in a UNIX environment. Some tools are provided for C programmers:

dbx

A symbolic debugger. Also *gdb, xxgdb ddd.*

make

A development tool for compiling large programs.

lex

A `lexer’. A program which generates C code to recognize words of text.

yacc

A `parser’. This is a tool which generates C code for checking the syntax of groups of textual words.

rpcgen

A protocol compiler which generates C code from a higher level language, for programming RPC applications.

Stdin, stdout, stderr

UNIX has three logical *streams* or *files* which are always open and are available to any program.

stdin

The standard input - file descriptor 0.

stdout

The standard output - file descriptor 1.

stderr

The standard error - file descriptor 2.

The names are a part of the C language and are defined as pointers of type FILE.

```
#include <stdio.h>
/* FILE *stdin, *stdout, *stderr; */
fprintf(stderr,”This is an error message!\n”);
```

The names are `logical’ in the sense that they do not refer to a particular device, or a particular place for information to come from or go. Their role is analogous to the `.’ and `..’ directories in the filesystem. Programs can write to these files without worrying about where the information comes from or goes to. The user can personally define these places by *redirecting standard I/O*. This is discussed in the next chapter.

A separate stream is kept for error messages so that error output does not get mixed up with a program’s intended output.

The superuser (root) and *nobody*

When logged onto a UNIX system directly, the user whose name is root has unlimited access to the files on the system. root can also become any other user without having to give a password. root is reserved for the system administrator or *trusted users*.

Certain commands are forbidden to normal users. For example, a regular user should not be able to halt the system, or change the ownership of files (see next paragraph). These things are reserved for the rootor *superuser*.

In a networked environment, root has no automatic authority on remote machines. This is to prevent the system administrator of one machine in Canada from being able to edit files on another in China. He or she must log in directly and supply a password in order to gain access privileges. On a network where files are often accessible in principle to anyone, the username root gets mapped to the user nobody, who has no rights at all.

The file hierarchy

UNIX has a hierarchical filesystem, which makes use of directories and sub-directories to form a tree. The root of the tree is called the root filesystem or `/'. Although the details of where every file is located differ for different versions of unix, some basic features are the same. The main sub-directories of the root directory together with the most important file are shown in the figure. Their contents are as follows.

`/bin'

Executable (binary) programs. On most systems this is a separate directory to /usr/ bin. In SunOS, this is a pointer (link) to /usr/bin.

`/etc'

Miscellaneous programs and configuration files. This directory has become very messy over the history of UNIX and has become a dumping ground for almost anything. Recent versions of UNIX have begun to tidy up this directory by creating subdirectories `/etc/mail', `/etc/services' etc!

`/usr'

This contains the main meat of UNIX. This is where application software lives, together with all of the basic libraries used by the OS.

`/usr/bin'

More executables from the OS.

`/usr/local'

This is where users' custom software is normally added.

`/sbin'

A special area for statically linked system binaries. They are placed here to distinguish commands used solely by the system administrator from user commands and so that they lie on the system root partition where they are guaranteed to be accessible during booting.

`/sys'

This holds the configuration data which go to build the system kernel. (See below.)

`/export'

Network servers only use this. This contains the disk space set aside for client machines which do not have their own disks. It is like a `virtual disk' for diskless clients.

`/dev, /devices'

A place where all the `logical devices' are collected. These are called `device nodes' in UNIX and are created by mknod. Logical devices are UNIX's official entry points for writing to devices. For instance,/dev/console is a route to the system console, while /dev/kmem is a route for reading kernel memory. Device nodes enable devices to be treated as though they were files.

`/home'

(Called */users* on some systems.) Each user has a separate login directory where files can be kept. These are normally stored under /home by some convention decided by the system administrator.

`/var›

System 5 and mixed systems have a separate directory for spooling. Under old BSD systems, /usr/spool contains spool queues and system data. /var/spool and /var/adm etc are used for holding queues and system log files.

`/vmunix›

This is the program code for the UNIX *kernel* (see below). On HPUX systems with file is called `hp-ux'. On linux it is called `linux'.

`/kernel›

On newer systems the kernel is built up from a number of modules which are placed in this directory.

Every UNIX directory contains two `virtual› directories marked by a single dot and two dots.

ls -a

. ..

The single dot represents the directory one is already in (the current directory). The double dots mean the directory one level up the tree from the current location. Thus, if one writes

cd /usr/local

cd ..

the final directory is /usr. The single dot is very useful in C programming if one wishes to read `the current directory›. Since this is always called `.› there is no need to keep track of what the current directory really is.

`.› and `..› are `hard links› to the true directories.

Symbolic links

A symbolic link is a pointer or an alias to another file. The command

ln -s fromfile /other/directory/tolink

makes the file fromfile appear to exist at /other/directory/tolink simultaneously. The file is not copied, it merely appears to be a part of the file tree in two places. Symbolic links can be made to both files and directories.

A symbolic link is just a small file which contains the name of the real file one is interested in. It cannot be opened like an ordinary file, but may be read with the C call readlink() See section lstat and readlink. If we remove the file a symbolic link points to, the link remains -- it just points nowhere.

Hard links

A *hard link* is a duplicate *inode* in the filesystem which is in every way equivalent to the original file inode. If a file is pointed to by a hard link, it cannot be removed until the link is removed. If a file has @math{n} hard links -- all of them must be removed before the file can be removed. The number of hard links to a file is stored in the filesystem *index node* for the file.

GETTING STARTED

If you have never met unix, or another multiuser system before, then you might find the idea daunting. There are several things you should know.

Logging in

Each time you use UNIX you must log on to the system by typing a username and a password. Your login name is sometimes called an `account' because some UNIX systems implement strict quotas for computer resources which have to be paid for with real money(2).

login: mark

password:

Once you have typed in your password, you are `logged on'. What happens then depends on what kind of system you are logged onto and how. If you have a colour monitor and keyboard in front of you, with a graphical user interface, you will see a number of windows appear, perhaps a menu bar. You then use a mouse and keyboard just like any other system.

This is not the only way to log onto unix. You can also log in remotely, from another machine, using the Secure Shell ssh program (this replaces the now antiquated telnet and rlogin programs). If you use these programs, you will normally only get a text or command line interface (though graphical interfaces can easily be arranged).

Once you have logged in, a short message will be printed (called Message of the Day or motd) and you will see the C-shell prompt: the name of the host you are logged onto followed by a percent sign, e.g.

Linux cube 2.2.19pre13 #2 Mon Feb 26 15:53:31 MET 2001 i686 unknown

```
    This is GNU/Linux - send problems to help@example.org
10:44pm  up 8 days, 13:34,  3 users,  load average: 0.08, 0.02, 0.01

  There are 480 messages in your incoming mailbox.
```

Remember that every UNIX machine is a separate entity: it is not like logging onto a PC system where you log onto the `network' i.e. the PC file server. Every UNIX machine is a server, or a client -- more correctly a "peer" (equal partner). The network, in unix-land, has lots of players.

The first thing you should do once you have logged on is to set a reliable password. A poor password might be okay on a PC which is not attached to a large network, but once you are attached to the Internet, you have to remember that the whole world will be trying to crack your password. Don't think that no one will bother: some people really have nothing better to do. A password should not contain any word that could be in a list of words (in any language), or be a simple concatenation of a word and a number (e.g. mark123). It takes seconds to crack such a password. Choose instead something which is easy to remember. Feel free to use the PIN number from your bankers card in your password! This will leave you with fewer things to remember. e.g. Ma9876rk). Passwords can be up to eight characters long.

Some sites allow you to change your password anywhere. Other sites require you to log onto a special machine to change your password:

```
dax%
dax% passwd
Change your password on host nexus
You cannot change it here
dax% rlogin nexus
password: ******

nexus% passwd
Changing password for mark
Enter login password: ********
Enter new password: ********
Reenter new passwd: ********
```

You will be prompted for your old password and your new password twice. If your network is large, it might take the system up to an hour or two to register the change in your password, so don't forget the old one right away!

Mouse buttons

UNIX has three mouse buttons. On some PC's running GNU/Linux or some other PC unix, there are only two, but the middle mouse button can be simulated by pressing both mouse buttons simultaneously. The mouse buttons have the following general functions. They may also have additional functions in special software.

index finger

This is used to select and click on objects. It is also used to mark out areas and copy by dragging. This is the button you normally use.

middle finger

Used to pull down menus. It is also used to paste a marked area somewhere at the mouse position.

outer finger

Pulls down menus.

On a left-handed system right and left are reversed.

E-mail

Reading electronic mail on UNIX is just like any other system, but there are many programs to choose from. There are very old programs from the seventies such as

mail

and there are fully graphical mail programs such as

tkrat

mailtool

Choose the program you like best. Not all of the programs support modern multimedia extensions because of their age. Some programs like tkrat have immediate mail notification alerts. To start a mail program you just type its name. If you have an icon-bar, you can click on the mail-icon.

Simple commands

Inexperienced computer users often prefer to use file-manager programs to avoid typing anything. With a mouse you can click your way through directories and files without having to type anything (e.g. thekfm or tkdesk programs). More experienced users generally find this to be slow and tedious after a while and prefer to use written commands. UNIX has many short cuts and keyboard features which make typed commands extremely fast and much more powerful than use of the mouse.

Today the CDE, KDE and GNOME projects are the most important efforts to write graphical user interfaces for computers. The CDE (Common Desktop Environment) is a commercial program developed by IBM, Hewlett-Packard, Sun Microsystems and many other vendors. KDE (a German effort, a pun on CDE) and GNOME are free software window systems which have taken windowing to the next level. While they have borrowed and stolen many ideas from Windows' innovative Windows 95 user interface, they have taken windowing beyond this.

If you come from a Windows environment, the UNIX commands can be a little strange. It is a different way of thinking: using language to ask for exactly what you want, instead of pointing to a menu of limited choices. It is also a strange language. Because they stem from an era when keyboards had to be hit with hammer force, and machines were very slow, the UNIX command names are as short as possible, so they seem pretty cryptic. Some familiar ones which DOS borrowed from UNIX include,

cd

mkdir

which change to a new directory and make a new directory respectively. To list the files in the current directory you use,

ls

To rename a file, you `move' it:

mv *old-name new-name*

Text editing and word processing

Text editing is one of the things which people spend most time doing on any computer. It is important to distinguish text editing from word processing. On a PC or MacIntosh, you are perhaps used to Word or WordPerfect for writing documents.

UNIX has a Word-like program called lyx, and even several Office clones (e.g. Star Office soffice), but for the most part UNIX users do not use word processors. It is more common in the UNIX community to write all documents, regardless of whether they are letters, books or computer programs, using a non-formatting text editor. (UNIX word processors like Framemaker do exist, but they are very expensive. A version of MS-Word also exists for some unices.) Once you have written a document in a normal text editor, you call up a text formatter to make it pretty. You might think this strange, but the truth of the matter is that this two-stage process gives you the most power and flexibility--and that is what most UNIX folks like.

For writing programs, or anything else, you edit a file by typing:

emacs myfile

emacs is one of dozens of text-editors. It is not the simplest or most intuitive, but it is the most powerful and if you are going to spend time learning an editor, it wouldn't do any harm to make it this one. You could also click on emacs' icon if you are relying on a window system. Emacs is almost certainly the most powerful text editor that exists on any system. It is not a word-processor, it is not for formatting printed documents, but it can be linked to almost any other program in order to format and print text. It contains a powerful programming language and has many intelligent features. We shall not go into the details of document formatting in this book, but only mention that programs like troff and Tex or Latex are used for this purpose to obtain typeset-quality printing. Text formatting is an area where UNIX folks do things differently to PC folks.

THE LOGIN ENVIRONMENT

UNIX began as a timesharing mainframe system in the seventies, when the only terminals available were text based *teletype* terminals or *tty*-s. Later, the Massachusetts Institute of Technology (MIT) developed the X-windows interface which is now a standard across UNIX platforms. Becausc of this history, the X-window system works as a front end to the standard UNIX shell and interface, so to understand the user environment we must first understand the shell.

Shells

A shell is a command interpreter. In the early days of UNIX, a shell was the only way of issuing commands to the system. Nowadays many window-based application programs provide menus and buttons to perform simple commands, but the UNIX shell remains the most powerful and flexible way of interacting with the system.

After logging in and entering a password, the UNIX process *init* starts a shell for the user logging in. UNIX has several different kinds of shell to choose from, so that each user can pick his/her favourite command interface. The type of shell which the system starts at login is determined by the user's entry in the *passwd* database. On most systems, the standard login shell is a variant of the C-shell.

Shells provide facilities and commands which

- Start and stop processes (programs)
- Allow two processes to communicate through a *pipe*
- Allow the user to redirect the flow of input or output
- Allow simple command line editing and command history
- Define aliases to frequently used commands
- Define global "environment" variables which are used to configure the default behaviour of a variety of programs. These lie in an "associated array" for each process and may be seen with the `env'command. Environment variables are inherited by all processes which are started from a shell.
- Provide wildcard expansion (joker notation) of filenames using `*,?,[]'
- Provide a simple script language, with tests and loops, so that users can combine system programs to create new programs of their own.
- Change and remember the location of the current working directory, or location within the file hierarchy.

The shell does not contain any more specific functions--all other commands, such as programs which list files or create directories etc., are executable programs which are independent of the shell. When you type `ls', the shell looks for the executable file called `ls' in a special list of directories called *the command path* (which is contained in the environment variable $PATH) and attempts to start this program. This allows such programs to be developed and replaced independently of the actual command interpreter.

Each shell which is started can be customized and configured by editing a setup file. For the Bash shell this file is called `.bashrc›, and for the C-shell and its variants it is called `.profile›. (Note that files which begin with leading dots are not normally visible with the `ls› command. Use `ls -a› to view these.) Any commands which are placed in these files are interpreted by the shell before the first command prompt is issued. These files are typically used to define a command search path and terminal characteristics.

On each new command line you can use the cursor keys to edit the line. The up-arrow browses back through earlier commands. CTRL-a takes you to the start of the line. CTRL-e takes you to the end of the line. The TAB can be used to save typing with the `completion' facility See section Command/filename completion.

Shell commands generally

Shell commands are commands like cp, mv, passwd, cat, more, less, cc, grep, ps etc..

One thing you can always bet on with UNIX is that there is not just one way of doing things -- there are so many standards, that there is often a bewildering array to choose from. UNIX has two main command shells. They are called sh (Bourne Shell) and csh C-shell. Their modern implementations are called Bash (Bourne Again Shell) and tcsh (T-C shell).

Very few commands are actually built into the shell command line interpreter, in the same way that they are built into DOS. Rather commands are programs which exist as actual program files. When we type a command, the shell searches for a program with the same name and tries to execute it. This is very flexible, since anyone is free to write their own programs and therefore extend the command language of the system. The file must be executable, or a Command not found error will result. To see what actually happens when you type a command like gcc, try typing the following into a GNU/Linux system: (you can type this exactly as shown into a Bash shell)

```
cube$ IFS=:
cube$ for dir in $PATH       # for every directory in the list path
>do
> if [ -x $dir/gcc ]      # if the file is executable
> then
>    echo Found $dir/gcc   # Print message found!
>    break                # break out of loop
> else
>    echo Searching $dir/gcc
> fi
>done
```

If you use C-shell (e.g. tcsh), try typing in the following C-shell commands *directly into a C-shell.*

```
nexus% foreach dir ( $path ) # for every directory in the list path
```

```
>   if ( -x $dir/gcc ) then   # if the file is executable
>     echo Found $dir/gcc     # Print message found!
>     break                   # break out of loop
>   else
>     echo Searching $dir/gcc
>   endif
> end
```

The output of these command sequences is something like this:

```
Searching /usr/lang/gcc
Searching /usr/openwin/bin/gcc
Searching /usr/openwin/bin/xview/gcc
Searching /physics/lib/framemaker/bin/gcc
Searching /physics/motif/bin/gcc
Searching /physics/mutils/bin/gcc
Searching /physics/common/scripts/gcc
Found /physics/bin/gcc
```

If you type

```
echo $PATH
```

in Bourne Shell, or

```
echo $path
```

in C-shell you will see the entire list of directories which are searched by the shell. If we had left out the `break' command, we might have discovered that UNIX often has several programs with the same name, in different directories! For example,

/bin/mail

/usr/ucb/mail

/bin/Mail

/bin/make

/usr/local/bin/make.

Also, different versions of UNIX have different conventions for placing the commands in directories, so the path list needs to be different for different types of UNIX machine. In Bash a few basic commands like cd and kill are built into the shell (as in DOS).

You can find out which directory a command is stored in using

type

command. For example

```
cube$ type cd
```

cd is a shell builtin

cube$ type mv

mv is /bin/mv

cube$

type only searches the directories in $PATH and quits after the first match, so if there are several commands with the same name, you will only see the first of them using type.

Finally, in the C-shell the command corresponding to type is built in and called which. In Bash which is a program:

cube$ type which

which is /usr/bin/which

cube$ tcsh

cube% which which

which: shell built-in command.

Take a look at the script /usr/bin/which. It is a script written in bash.

Environment and shell variables

Environment variables are variables which the shell keeps. They are normally used to configure the behaviour of utility programs like lpr (which sends a file to the printer) and mail (which reads and sends mail) so that special options do not have to be typed in every time you run these programs.

Any program can read these variables to find out how you have configured your working environment. We shall meet these variables frequently. Here are some important variables

PATH # The search path for shell commands (bash)

TERM # The terminal type (bash and csh)

DISPLAY # X11 - the name of your display

LD_LIBRARY_PATH # Path to search for object and shared libraries

HOSTNAME # Name of this UNIX host

PRINTER # Default printer (lpr)

HOME # The path to your home directory (bash)

PS1 # The default prompt for bash

path # The search path for shell commands (csh)

term # The terminal type (csh)

prompt # The default prompt for csh

home # The path to your home directory (csh)

These variables fall into two groups. Traditionally the first group always have names in uppercase letters and are called *environment variables*, whereas variables in the second group have names with lowercase letters and are called *shell variables*-- but this is only a convention. The uppercase variables are *global variables*, whereas the lower case variables are *local variables*. Local variables are not defined for programs or sub-shells started by the current shell, while global variables are inherited by all sub-shells.

The Bash-shell and the C-shell use these conventions differently and not always consistently. You will see how to define these below. For now you just have to know that you can use the command env can be used in Bash shell to see all of the defined global environment variables while set lists both the global and the local variables.

Wildcards

Sometimes you want to be able to refer to several files in one go. For instance, you might want to copy all files ending in `.c' to a new directory. To do this one uses *wildcards*. Wildcards are characters like * ?which stand for any character or group of characters. In card games the joker is a `wild card' which can be substituted for any other card. Use of wildcards is also called *filename substitution* in the UNIX manuals, in the sections on sh and csh.

The wildcard symbols are,

`?›

Match single character. e.g. ls /etc/rc.????

`*›

Match any number of characters. e.g. ls /etc/rc.*

`[...]›

Match any character in a list enclosed by these brackets. e.g. ls [abc].C

Here are some examples and explanations.

`/etc/rc.????›

Match all files in /etc whose first three characters are rc. and are 7 characters long.

`*.c›

Match all files ending in `.c› i.e. all C programs.

`*.[Cc]›

List all files ending on `.c› or `.C› i.e. all C and C++ programs.

`*.[a-z]›

Match any file ending in .a, .b, .c, ... up to .z etc.

It is important to understand that *the shell expands wildcards*. When you type a command, the program is not invoked with an argument that contains * or ?. The shell expands the special characters first and invokes commands with the entire list of files which match the patterns. The programs never see the wildcard characters, only the list of files they stand for. To see this in action, you can type echo /etc/rc*

which gives

/etc/rc0 /etc/rc0.d /etc/rc1 /etc/rc1.d /etc/rc2 /etc/rc2.d /etc/rc3

/etc/rc3.d /etc/rc5 /etc/rc6 /etc/rcS /etc/rcS.d

All shell commands are invoked with a command line of this form. This has an important corollary. It means that multiple renaming *cannot work*!

UNIX files are renamed using the mv command. In many microcomputer operating systems one can write

rename *.x *.y

which changes the file extension of all files ending in `.x' to the same name with a `.y' extension. This cannot work in UNIX, because the shell tries expands everything before passing the arguments to the command line.

Regular expressions

The wildcards belong to the shell. They are used for matching filenames. UNIX has a more general and widely used mechanism for matching *strings*, this is through *regular expressions*.

Regular expressions are used by the egrep utility, text editors like ed, vi and emacs and sed and awk. They are also used in the C programming language for matching input as well as in the Perl programming language and lex tokenizer. Here are some examples using the egrep command which print lines from the file /etc/rc which match certain conditions. The construction is part of egrep. Everything in between these symbols is a regular expression. Notice that special shell symbols ! * & have to be preceded with a backslash \ in order to prevent the shell from expanding them!

Print all lines beginning with a comment

egrep '(^#)' /etc/rc

Print all lines which DON'T begin with

egrep '(^[^#])' /etc/rc

Print all lines beginning with e, f or g.

egrep '(^[efg])' /etc/rc

Print all lines beginning with uppercase

egrep '(^[A-Z])' /etc/rc

Print all lines NOT beginning with uppercase

egrep '(^[^A-Z])' /etc/rc

Print all lines containing ! * &

egrep '([\!*\&])' /etc/rc

All lines containing ! * & but not starting

egrep '([^#][\!*\&])' /etc/rc

Regular expressions are made up of the following `atoms'.

These examples assume that the file `/etc/rc' exists. If it doesn't exist on the machine you are using, try to find the equivalent by, for instance, replacing /etc/rc with /etc/rc* which will try to find a match beginning with the rc.

`.'

Match any single character except the end of line.

`^'

Match the beginning of a line as the first character.

`$'

Match end of line as last character.

`[..]'

Match any character in the list between the square brackets.(see below).

`*'

Match zero or more occurrences of the preceding expression.

`+'

Match one or more occurrences of the preceding expression.

`?'

Match zero or one occurrence of the preceding expression.

You can find a complete list in the UNIX manual pages. The square brackets above are used to define a *class* of characters to be matched. Here are some examples,

- If the square brackets contain a list of characters, $[a-z156]$ then a single occurrence of any character in the list will match the regular expression: in this case any lowercase letter or the numbers 1, 5 and 6.
- If the first character in the brackets is the caret symbol `^› then any character *except* those in the list will be matched.
- Normally a dash or minus sign `-› means a range of characters. If it is the first character after the `[‹ or after `[^› then it is treated literally.

Nested shell commands and "

The backwards apostrophes `...` can be used in all shells and also in the programming language Perl. When these are encountered in a string the shell tries to execute the command inside the quotes and replace the quoted expression by the result of that command. For example:

UNIX$ echo "This system's kernel type is `/usr/bin/file /boot/vmlinuz-2.2.19pre13`"

This system's kernel type is /boot/vmlinuz-2.2.19pre13: Linux kernel x86 boot executable bzImage, version 2.2.19pre13

```
UNIX$ for file in `ls /local/ssl/misc/*`
> do
> echo I found a config file $file
> echo Its type is `/usr/bin/file $file`
> done
I found a config file /local/ssl/misc/CA.pl
Its type is /local/ssl/misc/CA.pl: perl script text
I found a config file /local/ssl/misc/CA.sh
Its type is /local/ssl/misc/CA.sh: Bourne shell script text
I found a config file /local/ssl/misc/c_hash
Its type is /local/ssl/misc/c_hash: Bourne shell script text
I found a config file /local/ssl/misc/c_info
Its type is /local/ssl/misc/c_info: Bourne shell script text
I found a config file /local/ssl/misc/c_issuer
Its type is /local/ssl/misc/c_issuer: Bourne shell script text
I found a config file /local/ssl/misc/c_name
Its type is /local/ssl/misc/c_name: Bourne shell script text
I found a config file /local/ssl/misc/der_chop
Its type is /local/ssl/misc/der_chop: perl script text
```

This is how we insert the result of a shell command into a text string or variable.

UNIX command overview

Important keys

TAB

The TAB key is used by Bash and Emacs for "filename completion", i.e. when you are uncertain of the correct name of something, or simply can't be bothered to type it out, you can hit TAB to either finish off the word, or show you alternative choices. e.g. try in Bash

```
cube$ loadTAB
loadkeys   loadmeter   loadunimap
```

This shows the possible completions of commands which match "load". Type one more letter and TAB, and the rest will be filled in.

CTRL-A

Jump to start of line. If `screen' is active, this prefixes all control key commands for `screen' and then the normal CTRL-A is replaced by CTRL-a a.

CTRL-C

Interrupt or break key. Sends signal 15 to a process.

CTRL-D

Signifies `EOF' (end of file) or shows expansion matches in command/filename completion See section Command/filename completion.

CTRL-E

Jump to end of line.

CTRL-L

Clear screen in newer shells and in emacs. Same as `clear' in the shell.

CTRL-Z

Suspend the present process, but do not destroy it. This sends signal 18 to the process.

Alternative shells

bash

The Bourne Again shell, an improved sh.

csh

The standard C-shell.

jsh

The same as sh, with C-shell style job control.

ksh

The Korn shell, an improved sh.

sh

The original Bourne shell.

sh5

On ULTRIX systems the standard Bourne shell is quite stupid. sh5 corresponds to the normal Bourne shell on these systems.

tcsh

An improved C-shell.

zsh

An improved sh.

Window based terminal emulators

xterm

The standard X11 terminal window.

shelltool, cmdtool

Openwindows terminals from Sun Microsystems. These are not completely X11 compatible during copy/paste operations.

screen

This is not a window in itself, but allows you to emulate having several windows inside a single (say) xterm window. The user can switch between different windows and open new ones, but can only see one window at a time See section Multiple screens.

Remote shells and logins

The best way to log onto another system is to use the Secure Shell command ssh. This replaces the now obsolete commands:

rlogin

Login onto a remote UNIX system.

rsh

Open a shell on a remote system (require access rights).

telnet

Open a connection to a remove system using the telnet protocol.

These old commands are insecure andnote very flexible. The Secure Shell offers encryption, strong authentication and greater functionality. It can be used to run a single program on a remote machine, or to login on the remote machine.

cube$ ssh metaverse date

cube$ ssh metaverse

Text editors

ed

An ancient line-editor.

vi

Visual interface to ed. This is the only "standard" UNIX text editor supplied by vendors.

emacs

The most powerful UNIX editor. A fully configurable, user programmable editor which works under X11 and on tty-terminals.

xemacs

A pretty version of emacs for X11 windows.

pico

A tty-terminal only editor, comes as part of the PINE mail package.

xedit

A test X11-only editor supplied with X-windows.

textedit

A simple X11-only editor supplied by Sun Microsystems.

File handling commands

ls

List files in specified directory (like dir on other systems).

cp

Copy files.

mv

Move or rename files.

touch

Creates an empty new file if none exists, or updates date and time stamps on existing files.

rm, unlink

Remove a file or link (delete).

mkdir, rmdir

Make or remove a directory. A directory must be empty in order to be able to remove it.

cat

Concatenate or join together a number of files. The output is written to the standard output by default. Can also be used to simply print a file on screen.

lp, lpr

Line printer. Send a file to the default printer, or the printer defined in the `PRINTER' environment variable.

lpq, lpstat

Show the status of the print queue.

File browsing

more

Shows one screen full at a time. Possibility to search for a string and edit the file. This is like `type *file* | more' in DOS.

less

An enhanced version of more.

mc

Midnight commander, a free version of the `Norton Commander› PC utility for UNIX. (Only for non-serious UNIX users...)

kfm

A window based file manager with icons and all that nonsense.

Ownership and granting access permission

chmod

Change file access mode.

chown, chgrp

Change owner and group of a file. The GNU version of chown allows both these operations to be performed together using the syntax chown *owner.group file*.

acl

On newer Unices, Access control lists allow access to be granted on a per-user basis rather than by groups.

Extracting from and rebuilding files

cut

Extract a column in a table

paste

Merge several files so that each file becomes a column in a table.

sed

A batch text-editor for searching, replacing and selecting text without human intervention.

awk

A prerunner to the Perl language, for extracting and modifying textfiles.

rmcr

Strip carriage return (ASCII 13) characters from a file. Useful for converting DOS files to UNIX.

Locating files

find

Search for files from a specified directory using various criteria.

locate

Fast search in a global file database for files containing a search-string.

whereis

Look for a command and its documentation on the system.

Disk usage.

du

Show number of blocks used by a file or files.

df

Show the state of usage for one or more disk partitions.

Show other users logged on

users

Simple list of other users.

finger

Show who is logged onto this and other systems.

who

List of users logged into this system.

w

Long list of who is logged onto this system and what they are doing.

Contacting other users

write

Send a simple message to the named user, end with CTRL-D. The command `mesg n' switches off messages receipt.

talk

Interactive two-way conversation with named user.

irc

Internet relay chat. A conferencing system for realtime multi-user conversations, for addicts and losers.

Mail senders/readers

mail

The standard (old) mail interface.

Mail

Another mail interface.

elm

Electronic Mail program. Lots of functionality but poor support for multimedia.

pine

Rumours (untrue) are that pine stands for Pine is Not Elm; it actually stands for nothing at all. Improved support for multimedia but very slow and rather stupid at times. Some of the best features of elm have been removed!

mailtool

Sun's openwindows client program.

rmail

A mail interface built into the emacs editor.

netscape mail

A mail interface built into the netscape navigator.

zmail

A commercial mail package.

tkrat

A graphical mail reader which supports most MIME types, written in tcl/tk. This program has a nice feel and allows you to create a searchable database of old mail messages, but has a hopeless locking mechanism.

File transfer

ftp

The File Transfer program - copies files to/from a remote host.

ncftp

An enhanced ftp for anonymous login.

Compilers

cc

The C compiler.

CC

The C++ compiler.

gcc

The GNU C compiler.

g++

The GNU C++ compiler.

javac

A generator of Java bytecode.

java

A Java Virtual Machine.

ld

The system linker/loader.

ar

Archive library builder.

dbx

A symbolic debugger.

gdb

The GNU symbolic debugger.

xxgdb

The GNU debugger with a window driven front-end.

ddd

A motif based front-end to the gdb debugger.

Other interpreted languages

perl

Practical extraction an report language.

tcl

A perl-like language with special support for building user interfaces and command shells.

php

Personal Home Page Tools (officially "PHP: Hypertext Preprocessor"). A server-side HTML-embedded scripting language.

scheme

A lisp-like extensible scripting language from GNU.

mercury

A prolog-like language for artificial intelligence.

Processes and system statistics

ps

List system process table.

vmstat

List kernel virtual-memory statistics.

netstat

List network connections and statistics.

rpcinfo

Show rpc information.

showmount

Show clients mounting local filesystems.

System identity

uname

Display system name and operating system release.

hostname

Show the name of this host.

domainname

Show the name of the local NIS domain. Normally this is chosen to be the same as the BIND/DNS domain, but it need not be.

nslookup

Interrogate the DNS/BIND name service (hostname to IP address conversion).

Internet resources

archie, xarchie

Search the internet ftp database for files.

xrn, fnews

Read news (browser).

netscape, xmosaic

Read world wide web (WWW) (browser).

Text formatting and postscript

tex, latex

Donald Knuth's text formatting language, pronounced "tek" (the x is really a Greek "chi"). Used widely for technical publications. Compiles to dvi (device independent) file format.

texinfo

A hypertext documentation system using tex and "info" format. This is the GNU documentation system. This UNIX guide is written in texinfo!!!

xdvi

View a tex dvi file on screen.

dvips

Convert dvi format into postscript.

ghostview, ghostscript

View a postscript file on screen.

Picture editors and processors

xv

Handles, edits and processes pictures in a variety of standard graphics formats (gif, jpg, tiff etc). Use xv -quit to place a picture on your root window.

xpaint

A simple paint program.

xfig

A line drawing figure editor. Produces postscript, tex, and a variety of other output formats.

xmgr

A graphing and analysis program.

xsetroot

Load an X-bitmap image into the screen (root window) background. Small images are tiled.

Miscellaneous

date

Print the date and time.

ispell

Spelling checker.

xcalc

A graphical calculator.

dc,bc

Text-based calculators.

xclock

A clock!

ping

Send a “sonar” ping to see if another UNIX host is alive.

Terminals

In order to communicate with a user, a shell needs to have access to a terminal. UNIX was designed to work with many different kinds of terminals. Input/output commands in UNIX read and write to a virtual terminal. In *reality* a terminal might be a text-based Teletype terminal (called a *tty* for short) or a graphics based terminal; it might be 80-characters wide or it might be wider or narrower. UNIX take into account these possibility by defining a number of instances of terminals in a more or less object oriented way.

Each user›s terminal has to be configured before cursor based input/output will work correctly. Normally this is done by choosing one of a number of standard terminal types a list which is supplied by the system. In practice the user defines the value of the environment variable `TERM› to an appropriate name. Typical examples are `vt100› and `xterm›. If no standard setup is found, the terminal can always be configured manually using UNIX›s most cryptic and opaque of commands: `stty›.

The job of configuring terminals is much easier now that hardware is more standard. Users› terminals are usually configured centrally by the system administrator and it is seldom indeed that one ever has to choose anything other than `vt100› or `xterm›.

The X window system

Because UNIX originated before windowing technology was available, the user-interface was not designed with windowing in mind. The X window system attempts to be like a virtual machine park, running a different program in each window. Although the programs appear on one screen, they may in fact be running on UNIX systems anywhere in the world, with only the output being local to the user's display. The standard shell interface is available by running an X client application called `xterm' which is a graphical front-end to the standard UNIX textual interface.

The `xterm' program provides a virtual terminal using the X windows graphical user interface. It works in exactly the same way as a *tty* terminal, except that standard graphical facilities like copy and paste are available. Moreover, the user has the convenience of being able to run a different shell in every window. For example, using the `rlogin' command, it is possible to work on the local system in one window, and on another remote system in another window. The X-window environment allows one to cut and paste between windows, regardless of which host the shell runs on.

The components of the X-window system

The X11 system is based on the client-server model. You might wonder why a window system would be based on a model which was introduced for interprocess communication, or network communication. The answer is straightforward.

The designers of the X window system realized that network communication was to be the paradigm of the next generation of computer systems. They wanted to design a system of windows which would enable a user to sit at a terminal in Massachusetts and work on a machine in Tokyo -- and still be able to get high quality windows displayed on their terminal. The aim of X windows from the beginning is to create a *distributed* window environment.

When I log onto my friend›s Hewlett Packard workstation to use the text editor (because I don›t like the one on my EUNUCHS workstation) I want it to work correctly on my screen, with my keyboard -- even though my workstation is manufactured by a different company. I also want the colours to be right despite the fact that the HP machine uses a completely different video hardware to my machine. When I press the curly brace key {, I want to see a curly brace, and not some hieroglyphic because the HP station uses a different keyboard.

These are the problems which X tries to address. In a network environment we need a *common window system* which will work on any kind of hardware, and hide the differences between different machines as far as possible. But it has to be flexible enough to allow us to change all of the things we don't like -- to choose our own colours, and the kind of window borders we want etc. Other windowing systems (like Microsoft windows) ignore these problems and thereby lock the user to a single vendors products and a single operating system. (That, of course, is no accident.)

The way X solves this problem is to use the client server model. Each program which wants to open a window on somebody›s compute screen is a client of the *X window service*. To get something drawn on a user's screen, the client asks a server on the host of interest to draw windows for it. No client ever draws anything itself -- it asks the server to do it on its behalf. There are several reasons for this:

- The clients can all talk a common `window language' or *protocol*. We can hide the difference between different kinds of hardware by making the *machine-specific* part of drawing graphics entirely a problem of implementing the server on the particular hardware. When a new type of hardware comes along, we just need to modify the server -- none of the clients need to be modified.
- We can contact different servers and send our output to different hardware -- thus even though a program is running on a CPU in Tokyo, it can ask the server in Massachusetts to display its window for it.
- When more than one window is on a user›s display, it eventually becomes necessary to move the windows around and then figure out which windows are on top of which other windows etc. If all of the drawing information is kept in a server, it is straightforward to work out this information. If every client drew where it wanted to, it would be impossible to know which window was supposed to be on top of another.

In X, the window manager is a different program to the server which does the drawing of graphics -- but the client-server idea still applies, it just has one more piece to its puzzle.

How to set up X windows

The X windows system is large and complex and not particularly user friendly. When you log in to the system, X reads two files in your home directory which decide which applications will be started what they will look like. The files are called

.Xsession

This file is a shell script which starts up a number of applications as background processes and exits by calling a window manager. Here is a simple example file

```
#!/bin/bash
#
# .xsession file
#
#

   PATH="/usr/bin:/bin:/local/gnu/bin:/usr/X11R6/bin"

#
# List applications here, with & at the end
# so they run in the background
#
 xterm -T NewTitle -sl 1000 -geometry 90x45+16+150 -sb &
 xclock &
 xbiff -geometry 80x80+510+0 &
 netscape -iconic&
# Start a window manager. Exec replaces this script with
# the fvwm process, so that it doesn't exist as a separate
# (useless) process.
 exec /local/bin/fvwm
```

.Xdefaults

This file specifies all of the resources which X programs use. It can be used to change the colours used by applications, or font types etc. The subject of X-resources is a large one and we don't have time for it here. Here is a simple example, which shows how you can make your over-bright xterm and emacs windows less bright grey shade.

```
xterm*background: LightGrey
Emacs*background: grey92
Xemacs*background: grey92
```

X displays and authority

In the terminology used by X11, every client program has to contact a *display* in order to open a window. A display is a virtual screen which is created by the X server on a particular host. X can create several separate displays on a given host, though most machines only have one.

When an X client program wants to open a window, it looks in the UNIX environment variable `DISPLAY› for the IP address of a host which has an X server it can contact. For example, if we wrote

DISPLAY=»myhost:0»

export DISPLAY

the client would try to contact the X server on `myhost› and ask for a window on display number zero (the usual display). If we wrote

DISPLAY=»198.112.208.35:0»

export DISPLAY

the client would try to open display zero on the X server at the host with the IP address `198.112.208.35›.

Clearly there must be some kind of security mechanism to prevent just anybody from opening windows on someone›s display. X has two such mechanisms:

xhost

This mechanism is now obsolete. The `xhost' command is used to define a list of hosts which are allowed to open windows on the user's display. It cannot distinguish between individual users. i.e. the command xhost yourhost would allow *anyone* using yourhost to access the local display. This mechanism is only present for backward compatibility with early versions of X windows. Normally one should use the command xhost - to exclude all others from accessing the display.

Xauthority

The Xauthority mechanism has replaced the xhost scheme. It provides a security mechanism which can distinguish individual users, not just hosts. In order for a user to open a window on a display, he/she must have a ticket--called a "magic cookie". This is a binary file called `.Xauthority' which is created in the user's home directory when he/she first starts the X-windows system. Anyone who does not have a recent copy of this file cannot open windows or read the display of the user's terminal. This mechanism is based on the idea that the user's home directory is available via NFS on all hosts he/she will log onto, and thus the owner of the display will always have access to the magic cookie, and will therefore always be able to open windows on the display. Other users must obtain a copy of the file in order to open windows there. The command xauth is an interactive utility used for controlling the contents of the `.Xauthority' file. See the `xauth' manual page for more information.

Multiple screens

The window paradigm has been very successful in many ways, but anyone who has used a window system knows that the screen is simply not big enough for all the windows one would like! UNIX has several solutions to this problem.

One solution is to attach several physical screens to a terminal. The X window system can support any number of physical screens of different types. A graphical designer might want a high resolution colour screen for drawing and a black and white screen for writing text, for instance. The disadvantage with this method is the cost of the hardware.

A cheaper solution is to use a window manager such as `fwvm' which creates a virtual screen of unlimited size on a single monitor. As the mouse pointer reaches the edge of the true screen, the window manager replaces the display with a new "blank screen" in which to place windows. A miniaturized image of the windows on a control panel acts as a map which makes it possible to find the applications on the virtual screen.

Yet another possibility is to create virtual displays inside a single window. In other words, one can collapse several shell windows into a single `xterm' window by running the program `screen'. The screen command allows you to start several shells in a single window (using CTRL-a CTRL-c) and to switch between them (by typing CTRL-a CTRL-n). It is only possible to see one shell window at a time, but it is still possible to cut and paste between windows and one has a considerable saving of space. The `screen' command also allows you to suspend a shell session, log out, log in again later and resume the session precisely where you left off.

Here is a summary of some useful screen commands:

screen

Start the screen server.

screen -r

Resume a previously suspended screen session if possible.

CTRL-a CTRL-c

Start a new shell on top of the others (a fresh `screen') in the current window.

CTRL-a CTRL-n

Switch to the next `screen'.

CTRL-a CTRL-a

Switch to the last screen used.

CTRL-a a

When screen is running, CTRL-a is used for screen commands and cannot therefore be used in its usual shell meaning of `jump to start of line'. CTRL-a a replaces this.

CTRL-a CTRL-d

Detach the screen session from the current window so that it can be resumed later. It can be resumed with the `screen -r' command.

CTRL-a ?

Help screen.

FILES AND ACCESS

To prevent all users from being able to access all files on the system, UNIX records information about *who* creates files and also who is allowed to access them later.

Each user has a unique *username* or *loginname* together with a unique *user id* or *uid*. The user id is a number, whereas the login name is a text string -- otherwise the two express the same information. A file belongs to user A if it is *owned* by user A. User A then decides whether or not other users can read, write or execute the file by setting the *protection bits* or the *permission* of the file using the command chmod.

In addition to user identities, there are groups of users. The idea of a group is that several named users might want to be able to read and work on a file, without other users being able to access it. Every user is a member of at least one group, called the *login group* and each group has both a textual name and a number (*group id*). The *uid* and *gid* of each user is recorded in the file /etc/passwd (See chapter 6). Membership of other groups is recorded in the file /etc/group or on some systems /etc/ logingroup.

Protection bits

The following output is from the command ls -lag executed on a SunOS type machine.

```
lrwxrwxrwx  1 root    wheel          7 Jun  1  1993 bin -> usr/bin
-r--r--r--  1 root    bin       103512 Jun  1  1993 boot
drwxr-sr-x  2 bin     staff      11264 May 11 17:00 dev
drwxr-sr-x 10 bin     staff       2560 Jul  8 02:06 etc
drwxr-sr-x  8 root    wheel        512 Jun  1  1993 export
drwx------  2 root    daemon       512 Sep 26  1993 home
-rwxr-xr-x  1 root    wheel     249079 Jun  1  1993 kadb
lrwxrwxrwx  1 root    wheel          7 Jun  1  1993 lib -> usr/lib
drwxr-xr-x  2 root    wheel       8192 Jun  1  1993 lost+found
drwxr-sr-x  2 bin     staff        512 Jul 23  1992 mnt
dr-xr-xr-x  1 root    wheel        512 May 11 17:00 net
drwxr-sr-x  2 root    wheel        512 Jun  1  1993 pcfs
drwxr-sr-x  2 bin     staff        512 Jun  1  1993 sbin
lrwxrwxrwx  1 root    wheel         13 Jun  1  1993 sys->kvm/sys
drwxrwxrwx  6 root    wheel        732 Jul  8 19:23 tmp
drwxr-xr-x 27 root    wheel       1024 Jun 14  1993 usr
drwxr-sr-x 10 bin     staff        512 Jul 23  1992 var
-rwxr-xr-x  1 root    daemon   2182656 Jun  4  1993 vmUNIX
```

The first column is a textual representation of the protection bits for each file. Column two is the number of hard links to the file (See exercises below). The third and fourth columns are the user name and group name and the remainder show the file size in bytes and the creation date. Notice that the directories /bin and /sys are symbolic links to other directories.

There are sixteen protection bits for a UNIX file, but only twelve of them can be changed by users. These twelve are split into four groups of three. Each three-bit number corresponds to one *octal* number.

The leading four invisible bits gives information about the type of file: is the file a *plain file*, a *directory* or a *link*. In the output from ls this is represented by a single character: -, d or l.

The next three bits set the so-called *s-bits* and *t-bit* which are explained below.

The remaining three groups of three bits set flags which indicate whether a file can be read `r›, written to `w› or executed `x› by (i) the user who created them, (ii) the other users who are in the group the file is marked with, and (iii) any user at all.

For example, the permission

Type Owner Group Anyone

d rwx r-x ---

tells us that the file is a directory, which can be read and written to by the owner, can be read by others in its group, but not by anyone else.

Note about directories. It is impossible to cd to a directory unless the x bit is set. That is, directories must be `executable' in order to be accessible.

Here are some examples of the relationship between binary, octal and the textual representation of file modes.

Binary	Octal	Text
001	1	x
010	2	w
100	4	r
110	6	rw-
101	5	r-x
-	644	rw-r--r--

It is well worth becoming familiar with the octal number representation of these permissions.

chmod

The chmod command changes the permission or *mode* of a file. Only the owner of the file or the superuser can change the permission. Here are some examples of its use. Try them.

make read/write-able for everyone

```
chmod a+w myfile
# add the ‹execute› flag for directory
chmod u+x mydir/
# open all files for everyone
chmod 755 *
# set the s-bit on my-dir›s group
chmod g+s mydir/
# descend recursively into directory opening all files
chmod -R a+r dir
```

Umask

When a new file gets created, the operating system must decide what default protection bits to set on that file. The variable umask decides this. umask is normally set by each user in his or her .cshrc file (see next chapter). For example

```
umask 077   # safe
umask 022   # liberal
```

According the UNIX documentation, the value of umask is `XOR'ed (exclusive `OR') with a value of 666 & umask for plain files or 777 & umask for directories in order to find out the standard protection. Actually this is not quite true: `umask' only removes bits, it never sets bits which were not already set in 666. For instance

umask	Permission
077	600 (plain)
077	700 (dir)
022	644 (plain)
022	755 (dir)

The correct rule for computing permissions is not XOR but `NOT AND'.

Making programs executable

A UNIX program is normally executed by typing its pathname. If the x execute bit is not set on the file, this will generate a `Permission denied' error. This protects the system from interpreting nonsense files as programs. To make a program executable for someone, you must therefore ensure that they can execute the file, using a command like

chmod u+x *filename*

This command would set execute permissions for the owner of the file;

chmod ug+x *filename*

would set execute permissions for the owner and for any users in the same group as the file. Note that script programs must also be readable in order to be executable, since the shell has the interpret them by reading.

chown and chgrp

These two commands change the ownership and the group ownership of a file. Only the superuser can change the ownership of a file on most systems. This is to prevent users from being able to defeat quota mechanisms. (On some systems, which do not implement quotas, ordinary users can give a file away to another user but not get it back again.) The same applies to group ownership.

Making a group

Normally users other than root cannot define their own groups. This is a weakness in UNIX from older times which no one seems to be in a hurry to change.

s-bit and t-bit (sticky bit)

The s and t bits have special uses. They are described as follows.

Octal	Text	Name
4000	chmod u+s	Setuid bit
2000	chmod g+s	Setgid bit
1000	chmod +t	Sticky bit

The effect of these bits differs for plain files and directories and differ between different versions of UNIX. You should check the manual page man sticky to find out about your system! The following is common behaviour.

For executable files, the setuid bit tells UNIX that *regardless of who runs the program* it should be executed with the permissions and rights of owner of the file. This is often used to allow normal users limited access to root privileges. A *setuid-root* program is executed as root for any user. The setgid bit sets the group execution rights of the program in a similar way.

In BSD UNIX, if the setgid bit is set on a directory then any new files created in that directory assume the group ownership of the parent directory and not the logingroup of the user who created the file. This is standard policy under system 5.

A directory for which the sticky bit is set restrict the deletion of files within it. A file or directory inside a directory with the t-bit set can only be deleted or renamed by its owner or the superuser. This is useful for directories like the mail spool area and / tmp which must be writable to everyone, but should not allow a user to delete another user›s files.

(Ultrix) If an executable file is marked with a sticky bit, it is held in the memory or system swap area. It does not have to be fetched from disk each time it is executed. This saves time for frequently used programs like ls.

(Solaris 1) If a non-executable file is marked with the sticky bit, it will *not* be held in the disk page cache -- that is, it is never copied from the disk and held in RAM but is written to directly. This is used to prevent certain files from using up valuable memory.

On some systems (e.g. ULTRIX), only the superuser can set the sticky bit. On others (e.g. SunOS) any user can create a sticky directory.

BOURNE AGAIN SHELL

The Bourne Again shell (Bash) is the command interpreter which you use to run programs and utilities. It contains a simple programming language for writing tailor-made commands, and allows you to join together UNIX commands with pipes. It is a configurable environment, and once you know it well, it is the most efficient way of working with UNIX.

The Bourne Again shell was written by the Free Software Foundation as a part of the GNU project and Bash is the default shell in most GNU/Linux distributions. Because of its command line editing features, it is much more efficient for interactive use than Bourne shell, the original UNIX shell. Most of the system scripts in UNIX are written in the Bourne shell. Although Bash includes many extensions and features not found in the Bourne shell, it maintains compatibility with it so that you can run Bourne shell scripts under Bash. On many GNU/Linux systems Bourne shell ('/bin/sh') is symbolically linked to Bash ('/bin/bash') so that the scripts that require the presence of the Bourne shell still run. If you want to write a platform independent shell script able to run on as many UNIX variants as possible, you should stick to Bourne shell syntax and avoid the Bash extensions.

`~/.bashrc' and `~/.bash_profile' files

When you log on to a GNU/Linux system and your login shell is defined in `/etc/passwd' to be Bash, it first executes commands in the `/etc/profile' file. It then searches for the `~/.bash_profile',`~/.bash_login' or `~/.profile' file, in this order, and executes commands in the first of these that is found and is readable. When a login exits, it executes commands in the `~/.bash_logout' file.

When you start an non-login interactive Bash shell, it only executes commands in the `~/.bashrc' file, if it exists and is readable. However, this shell inherits any environment (exported) variables from the parent shell, so environment variables set in `/etc/profile' and `~/.bash_profile' are passed onto the non-login shells and later to its subshells.

Here is a very simple example `~/.bashrc' file:

```
#
# .bashrc - read in by every bash that starts.
#
umask 077            # Set the default file creation mask
PATH="~/bin:$PATH"   # Inserts own bin directory first in PATH
```

```
PS1="`uname`:\h\$ " # prompt
PS2="\h > "         # prompt for foreach and while
PRINTER=myprinter

# Aliases are shortcuts to UNIX commands

alias h=history

alias ll="ls -l"

alias cp='cp -i'

alias rm='rm -i'

alias c='ssh cube'
```

In order to make sure your `~/.bashrc' file is read when logging on with ssh to another machine, you may start your `~/.bash_profile' file like this:

```
#

# .bash_profile - read in every login.

#

if [ -f ~/.bashrc ]
then
  source ~/.bashrc  # runs .bashrc as if they where
                    # typed into this file
fi
```

Variables and export

Shell variables are defined using the syntax

```
VARIABLE="username is"
myname="`whoami`"
```

It is important that there be no space between the variable and the equals sign. These variables are then referred to using the dollar `$' symbol.

```
$ echo "My $VARIABLE $myname"
My username is mark
```

When assigning values to variables the dollar symbol is never used. By default these variables are *local* - that is they will not be passed on to programs and sub-shells running under the current shell. To make them global (so that child processes will inherit them) we use the command

```
export VARIABLE
```

This adds the variable to the process *environment*. Under Bash (but not under the old Bourne shell) it is also possible to declare a variable to be global on a single line by

export GLOBALVAR="global"

The command

set -a

changes the default so that all variables, after the command are created *global*.

Arrays or lists are often simulated in Bourne shell by sandwiching the colon `:' symbol between items

PATH=/bin:/usr/bin:/etc:/local/bin:.

LD_LIBARAY_PATH=/usr/lib:/usr/openwin/lib:/local/lib

but there is no real facility for arrays in the Bourne shell. Note that the UNIX `cut' command can be used to extract the elements of the list. Loops can also read such lists directly See section Loops in Bash. However, Bash version 2.x supports arrays as seen in the next section.

The value of a variable is given by the dollar symbol. It is also possible to use *curly braces* around the variable name to `protect' the variable from interfering text. For example:

$ animal=worm

$ echo book$animal

bookworm

$ thing=book

$ echo $thingworm

(nothing..)

$ echo ${thing}worm

bookworm

Default values can be given to variables in the Bourne shell. The following commands illustrate this.

echo ${var-»No value set»}

echo ${var=»Octopus»}

echo ${var+»Forced value»}

echo ${var?»No such variable»}

The first of these prints out the contents of `$var›, if it is defined. If it is not defined the variable is substituted for the string «No value set». The value of `var› is not changed by this operation. It is only for convenience.

The second command has the same effect as the first, but here the value of `$var› is actually changed to «Octopus» if `$var› is not set.

The third version is slightly peculiar. If `$var› is *already* set, its value will be forced to be "Forced value", otherwise it is left undefined.

Finally the last instance issues an error message «No such variable» if `$var› is not defined.

In Bash 2.x it is possible to extract parts of the string a variable is set to using the construction ${variable:offset:length}| as shown in the next example.

var=»abcdefg»

middle=${var:2:3}

echo $middle

cde

An offset of 2 skips the first 2 characters and a string of length 3 is extracted from the middle of the string.

Bash arrays

The original Bourne shell does not have arrays. Bash version 2.x does have arrays, however. An array can be assigned from a string of words separated by whitespaces or the individual elements of the array can be set individually.

colours=(red white green)

colours[3]="yellow"

An element of the array must be referred to using curly braces.

echo ${colours[1]}

white

Note that the first element of the array has index 0. The set of all elements is referred to by ${colours[*]}.

echo ${colours[*]}

red white green yellow

echo ${#colours[*]}

4

As seen the number of elements in an array is given by ${#colours[*]}.

Stdin, stdout, stderr and redirection to and from files

When the shell starts up, it inherits three files: `stdin', `stdout', and `stderr'. Standard input normally comes from the keyboard. Standard output and standard error normally go to the screen. There are times you want to read input from a file or send output of errors to a file. This can be accomplished by using *I/O redirection*.

In Bash and the Bourne shell, the standard input/output files are referred to by numbers rather than by names.

stdin

File number 0

stdout

File number 1

stderr

File number 2

The default routes for these files can be changed by redirection. The output of the command echo is by default sent to the screen, that is the stdout with file number 1 is sent to the screen. Using redirection operators it is possible to redirect the standard out of echo to where we want it. We can send output to a file with the following command.

echo “should be sent to a file” > file.txt

This creates a new file `file.txt’ containing the string ‘should be sent to a file’. The redirection operator could have been given as 1>, but it is understood that standard out is meant when skipping the number of the file handle. The single ‘>’ always creates a new file, while ‘>>’ appends to the end of a file.

If you had mistyped the command echo the result would have been:

ehco “should be sent to a file” > file.txt

bash: ehco: command not found

The standard error with file handle 2 is by default sent to the screen, independent of where standard out (1) is sent. If you like you can redirect stdout to another or the same file.

ehco “should be sent to a file” > file.txt 2> error.txt

cat error.txt

bash: ehco: command not found

There are several ways to send stderr to the same file as stdin is redirected to. The following three commands are equivalent.

ehco “should be sent to a file” >& file.txt

ehco “should be sent to a file” > file.txt 2> file.txt

ehco “should be sent to a file” > file.txt 2>&1

The string 2>&1 means that stderr(2) should be sent to the same file as stdout(1). This is the only why to do this under the Bourne shell and this construction is therefore often seen in system shell scripts.

Furthermore it is possible to force a command which by default takes standard input from the keyboard, to read input from a file by redirecting stdin. The mail-command expects input from keyboard, but the ‘<’ redirection operator makes it send the password file to the user mark:

/bin/mail mark < /etc/passwd

The following table summarizes the most important redirection operators:

Redirection operator What it does

<	Redirects input
>	Redirects output
>>	Appends output
2>	Redirects error
>&	Redirects output and error (Bash only)
2>&1	Redirects error where output (1) is going

Pipes

A *pipe* takes the output from the command on the left-hand side of the pipe symbol and sends it to the input of the command on the right-hand side of the pipe symbol. A pipeline can consist of several pipes and this makes pipes a very powerful tool. It enables us to combine all the small and efficient UNIX commands in any thinkable way. If you want to count the number of people logged on, you could save the output of the command who in the temporary file `tmp', use wc -l to count the number of lines in `tmp' and finally remove the temporary file.

```
$ who > tmp
$ wc -l tmp
    4 tmp
$ rm tmp
```

Using a pipe saves disk space and time: the stdout from who can be redirected to the stdin of wc -l through a pipe and there is no need for temporarily storing the output from who.

```
$ who | wc -l
    4
```

Most UNIX-commands are constructed with piping in mind and this makes it possible to solve complex tasks easily, by joining commands along a pipeline. Consider the following pipeline:

```
cat big.jpg | djpeg | pnmscale -pixels 150000 | cjpeg > small.jpg
```

The command cat sends the large JPEG-image to djpeg which decompresses it and sends the resulting bitmap to stdout. The stream of data floats through the next pipe to pnmscale which scales the bitmap image down to the given size. The scaled image is piped to the command cjpeg which compresses the standard input and finally produces a JPEG-image of reduced size which is stored in the file `small.jpg›.

Command history

The history feature in Bash means that you do not have to type commands over and over again. You can use the UP ARROW key to browse back through the list of commands you have typed previously and the keys LEFT ARROW and RIGHT ARROW to edit these commands.

In addition there are a couple of commands which selects commands from the history list.

`!!'

Execute the last command again.

`!4'

Execute command number 4.

The first of these simply repeats the last command. The second command gives an absolute number. The absolute command number can be seen by typing `history'.

Command/filename completion

In Bash you can save hours worth of typing errors by using the completion mechanism. This feature is based on the TAB key.

The idea is that if you type half a filename and press TAB, the shell will try to guess the remainder of the filename. It does this by looking at the files which match what you have already typed and trying to fill in the rest. If there are several files which match, the shell sounds the "bell" or beeps. You can then type TAB twice to obtain a list of the possible alternatives. Here is an example: suppose you have just a single file in the current directory called `very_long_filename', typing

more TAB

results in the following appearing on the command line

more very_long_filename

The shell was able to identify a unique file. Now suppose that you have two files called `very_long_filename' and `very_big_filename', typing

more TAB

results in the following appearing on the command line

more very_

and the shell beeps, indicating that the choice was not unique and a decision is required. Next, you type TAB twice(3) to see which files you have to choose from and the shell lists them and returns you to the command line, exactly where you were. You now choose `very_long_filename' by typing `l'. This is enough to uniquely identify the file. Pressing the TAB key again results in

more very_long_filename

on the screen. As long as you have written enough to select a file uniquely, the shell will be able to complete the name for you.

Completion also works on shell commands, but it is a little slower since the shell must search through all the directories in the command path to complete commands.

Single and double quotes

Two kinds of quotes can be used in shell apart from the backward quotes we mentioned above. The essential difference between them is that certain shell commands work inside *double* quotes but not inside single quotes. For example

cube$ echo /etc/rc*

/etc/rc.boot /etc/rc0.d /etc/rc1.d /etc/rc2.d /etc/rc3.d /etc/rc4.d

cube$ echo «/etc/rc*»

/etc/rc*

cube$ echo «`whoami` -- my name is $USER»

mark -- my name is mark

cube$ echo ‹`whoami` -- my name is $USER›

`whoami` -- my name is $USER

We see that the single quotes prevent *variable substitution* and *sub-shells*. Wildcards do not work inside either single or double quotes.

Job control, break key, `fg', `bg'

So far we haven't mentioned UNIX's ability to multitask. In the Bourne shell (`sh') there are no facilities for controlling several user processes. Bash provides some commands for starting and stopping processes. These originate from the days before windows and X11, so some of them may seem a little old-fashioned. They are still very useful nonetheless.

Let's begin by looking at the commands which are true for any shell. Most programs are run in the *foreground* or *interactively*. That means that they are connected to the standard input and send their output to the standard output. A program can be made to run in the background, if it does not need to use the standard I/O. For example, a program which generates output and sends it to a file could run in the background. In a window environment, programs which create their own windows can also be started as background processes, leaving standard I/O in the shell free.

Background processes run independently of what you are doing in the foreground.

UNIX Processes and BSD signals

A background process is started using the special character `&' at the end of the command line.

find / -name '*lib*' -print >& output &

The final `&' on the end of this line means that the job will be run in the background. Note that this is not confused with the redirection operator `>&' since it must be the last character on the line. The command above looks for any files in the system containing the string `lib' and writes the list of files to a file called `output'. This might be a useful way of searching for missing libraries which you want to include in your environment variable `LD_LIBRARY_PATH'. Searching the entire disk from the root directory `/' could take a long time, so it pays to run this in the background.

If we want to see what processes are running, we can use the `ps' command. `ps' without any arguments lists all of your processes, i.e. all processes owned by the user name you logged in with in the current shell. `ps' takes many options, for instance `ps auxg' will list all processes in gruesome detail (The "g" is for group, not gruesome!). `ps' reads the kernel's process tables directly.

Processes can be stopped and started, or killed one and for all. The `kill' command does this. There are, in fact, two versions of the `kill' command. One of them is built into Bash and the other is not. If you use Bash then you will never care about the difference. We shall nonetheless mention the special features of Bash built-ins below. The kill command takes a number called a *signal* as an argument and another number called the *process identifier* or *PID* for short. Kill send signals to processes. Some of these are fatal and some are for information only. The two commands

```
kill -15 127
kill 127
```

are identical. They both send signal 15 to PID 127. This is the normal *termination* signal and it is often enough to stop any process from running.

Programs can choose to ignore certain signals by trapping signals with a special handler. One signal they cannot ignore is signal 9.

```
kill -9 127
```

is a sure way of killing PID 127. Even though the process dies, it may not be removed from the kernel›s process table if it has a parent (see next section).

Here is the complete list of signals which the Linux kernel send to processes in different circumstances.

```
#define SIGHUP    1    /* Hangup (POSIX). */
#define SIGINT    2    /* Interrupt (ANSI). */
#define SIGQUIT   3    /* Quit (POSIX). */
#define SIGILL    4    /* Illegal instruction (ANSI). */
#define SIGTRAP   5    /* Trace trap (POSIX). */
#define SIGABRT   6    /* Abort (ANSI). */
#define SIGIOT    6    /* IOT trap (4.2 BSD). */
#define SIGBUS    7    /* BUS error (4.2 BSD). */
#define SIGFPE    8    /* Floating-point exception (ANSI). */
#define SIGKILL   9    /* Kill, unblockable (POSIX). */
#define SIGUSR1   10   /* User-defined signal 1 (POSIX). */
```

```
#define SIGSEGV    11     /* Segmentation violation (ANSI). */
#define SIGUSR2    12     /* User-defined signal 2 (POSIX). */
#define SIGPIPE    13     /* Broken pipe (POSIX). */
#define SIGALRM    14     /* Alarm clock (POSIX). */
#define SIGTERM    15     /* Termination (ANSI). */
#define SIGSTKFLT  16     /* Stack fault. */
#define SIGCLD     SIGCHLD /* Same as SIGCHLD (System V). */
#define SIGCHLD    17     /* Child status has changed (POSIX). */
#define SIGCONT    18     /* Continue (POSIX). */
#define SIGSTOP    19     /* Stop, unblockable (POSIX). */
#define SIGTSTP    20     /* Keyboard stop (POSIX). */
#define SIGTTIN    21     /* Background read from tty (POSIX). */
#define SIGTTOU    22     /* Background write to tty (POSIX). */
#define SIGURG     23     /* Urgent condition on socket (4.2 BSD). */
#define SIGXCPU    24     /* CPU limit exceeded (4.2 BSD). */
#define SIGXFSZ    25     /* File size limit exceeded (4.2 BSD). */
#define SIGVTALRM  26     /* Virtual alarm clock (4.2 BSD). */
#define SIGPROF    27     /* Profiling alarm clock (4.2 BSD). */
#define SIGWINCH   28     /* Window size change (4.3 BSD, Sun). */
#define SIGPOLL    SIGIO  /* Pollable event occurred (System V). */
#define SIGIO      29     /* I/O now possible (4.2 BSD). */
#define SIGPWR     30     /* Power failure restart (System V). */
#define SIGSYS     31     /* Bad system call. */
```

We have already mentioned 15 and 9 which are the main signals for users. Signal 1, or `HUP› can be sent to certain programs by the superuser. For instance

```
kill -1   <inetd>
kill -HUP <inetd>
```

which forces `inetd› to reread its configuration file. Sometimes it is useful to *suspend* a process temporarily and then *restart* it later.

```
kill -20 <PID>     # suspend process <PID>
kill -18 <PID>     # resume process <PID>
```

Child Processes and zombies

When you start a process from a shell, regardless of whether it is a background process or a foreground process, the new process becomes a *child* of the original shell. Remember that the shell is just a UNIX process itself. Moreover, if one of the children starts a new process then it will be a child of the child (a grandchild?)! Processes therefore form *hierarchies*. Several children can have a common *parent*.

If we kill a parent, then (unless the child has detached itself from the parent) all of its children die too. If a child dies, the parent is not affected. Sometimes when a child is killed, it does not die but becomes "defunct" or a zombie process. This means that the child has a parent which is *waiting* for it to finish. If the parent has not yet been informed that the child has died, for example because it has been suspended itself, then the dead child is not removed from the kernel's process table. When the parent wakes up and receives the message that the child has terminated, the process entry for the dead child can be removed.

Bash builtins: `jobs›, `kill›, `fg›,`bg›, break key

Now let's look at some commands which are built into Bash for starting and stopping processes. Bash refers to user programs as `jobs' rather than processes -- but there is no real difference. The added bonus of Bash is that each shell has a *job number* in addition to its PID. The job numbers are simpler and are private for the shell, whereas the PIDs are assigned by the kernel and are often very large numbers which are difficult to to remember. When a command is executed in the shell, it is assigned a job number. If you never run any background jobs then there is only ever one job number: 1, since every job exits before the next one starts. However, if you run background tasks, then you can have several jobs "active" at any time. Moreover, by *suspending* jobs, Bash allows you to have several interactive programs running on the same terminal -- the `fg' and `bg' commands allow you to move commands from the background to the foreground and vice-versa.

Take a look at the following shell session.

```
cube$ emacs myfile&
[3] 771
cube$
 ( other commands ... , edit myfile and close emacs )
```

When a background job is done, the shell prints a message at a suitable moment between prompts.

```
[3]+  Done                emacs myfile
cube$
```

This tells you that job number 1 finished normally. If the job exits abnormally then the word `Done› may be replaced by some other message. For instance, if you kill the job, it will say

```
cube$ kill %3
cube$
[3]+  Terminated          emacs myfile
cube$
```

You can list the jobs you have running using the `jobs› command. The output looks something like

```
cube$ jobs
[1]  Terminated      xdvi unix
[2]  Running         xemacs unix.texinfo &
[3]  Running         xterm -sb -sl 10000 &
[4]  Running         ghostview &
[5]  Running         netscape &
[6]  Running         xterm -sb -sl 10000 &
[7]  Running         xemacs fil &
[8]+ Stopped         emacs unix.log
[9]- Running         gimp &
```

To suspend a program which you are running in the foreground you can type CTRL-z (this is like sending a `kill -20› signal from the keyboard). (4) You can suspend any number of programs and then restart them one at a time using `fg' and `bg'. If you want job 5 to be restarted in the foreground, you would type

```
fg %5
```

When you have had enough of job 5, you can type CTRL-z to suspend it and then type

```
fg %6
```

to activate job 6. Provided a job does not want to send output to `stdout›, you can restart any job in the background, using a command like.

```
bg %4
```

This method of working was useful before windows were available. Using `fg› and `bg›, you can edit several files or work on several programs without have to quit to move from one to another.

See also some related commands for batch processing `at', `batch' and `atq', `cron'.

NOTE: CTRL-c sends a `kill -2' signal, which send a standard interrupt message to a program. This is always a safe way to interrupt a shell command.

Arithmetic in Bash

In Bourne shell arithmetic is performed entirely `by proxy'. To evaluate an expression we call the `expr' command or the `bc' precision calculator. Here are some examples of `expr'

```
a=`expr $a+1`              # increment a
a=`expr 4 + 10 \* 5`        # 4+10*5
check = `expr $a \> $b`     # true=1, false=0. True if $a > $b
```

`expr' is very sensitive to spaces and backslash characters and this makes it a bit awkward to do arithmetic under the Bourne shell.

Bash 2.0 provides a new and simpler way to do arithmetic using double parentheses. If you surround any integer arithmetic expression as in ((x = y + 1)), you can perform most arithmetic operations with the same syntax as in Java and C.

```
(( x = 1 ))
echo $x
1
(( x++ ))
(( y = 4*x ))
echo $y
8
```

Note that you do not need to use the dollar symbol to refer to a variable within the double parentheses (but you may do it) and that spaces are allowed.

```
(( sum = 2 ))
(( total = 4*$sum + sum ))
echo $total
10
```

The variables within double parentheses are throughout treated as integers. Assigning a float value like 2.5 to a variable results in an syntax error while assigning a string to a variable cause the string to be stored as zero.

Scripts and arguments

Scripts are created by making an executable file which begins with the sequence of characters

```
#!/bin/bash
```

This construction is quite general: any executable file which begins with a sequence

```
#!myprogram -option
```

will cause the shell to attempt to execute

```
myprogam -option filename
```

where *filename* is the name of the file.

If a script is to accept arguments then these can be referred to as ` $1 $2 $3..$9›. There is a logical limit of nine arguments to a Bourne script, but Bash handles the next arguments as `${10}›. `$0› is the name of the script itself.

Here is a simple Bash script which prints out all its arguments.

```
#!/bin/bash
#
# Print all arguments (version 1)
```

```
#

for arg in $*
do
  echo Argument $arg
done
echo Total number of arguments was $#
```

The `$*› symbol stands for the entire list of arguments and `$#› is the total number of arguments.

Another way of achieving the same is to use the `shift› command. We shall meet this again in the Perl programming language. `shift› takes the first argument from the argument list and deletes it, moving all of the other arguments down one number -- this is how we can handle long lists of arguments in the Bourne shell.

```
#!/bin/bash
#
# Print all arguments (version 2)
#

while ( true )
do
  arg=$1;
  shift;
  echo $arg was an argument;
  if [ $# -eq 0 ]; then
    break
  fi
done
```

Return codes

All programs which execute in UNIX return a value through the C `return' command. There is a convention that a return value of zero (0) means that everything went well, whereas any other value implies that some error occurred. The return value is usually the value returned in `errno', the external error variable in C.

Shell scripts can test for these values either by placing the command directly inside an `if' test, or by testing the variable `$?' which is always set to the return code of the last command. Some examples are given following the next two sections.

Tests and conditionals

Bash and the Bourne shell has an array of tests. They are written as follows. Notice that `test' is itself not a part of the shell, but is a program which works out conditions and provides a return code. See the manual page on `test' for more details.

test -f *file*

True if the file is a plain file

test -d *file*

True if the file is a directory

test -r *file*

True if the file is readable

test -w *file*

True if the file is writable

test -x *file*

True if the file is executable

test -s *file*

True if the file contains something

test -g *file*

True if setgid bit is set

test -u *file*

True if setuid bit is set

test s1 = s2

True if strings s1 and s2 are equal

test s1 != s2

True if strings s1 and s2 are unequal

test *x* -eq *y*

True if the integers *x* and *y* are numerically equal

test *x* -ne *y*

True if integers are not equal

test *x* -gt *y*

True if *x* is greater than *y*

test *x* -lt *y*

True if *x* is less than *y*

test *x* -ge *y*

True if *x*>=*y*

test *x* -le *y*

True if $x <= y$

!

Logical NOT operator

-a

Logical AND

-o

Logical OR

Note that an alternate syntax for writing these commands if to use the square brackets, instead of writing the word test.

[$x -lt $y] "==" test $x -lt $y

Just as with the arithmetic expressions, Bash 2.x provides a syntax for conditionals which are more similar to Java and C. While arithmetic C-like expressions can be used within double parentheses, C-like tests can be used within double square brackets.

[[$var == "OK" || $var == "yes"]]

This C-like syntax is not allowed in the Bourne shell, but is equivalent to

[$var = "OK" -o $var = "yes"]

which is valid in both shells.

Arithmetic C-like tests can be used within double parentheses so that under Bash 2.x the following tests are equivalent:

[$x -lt $y] "==" ((x < y))

Conditional structures

The conditional structures have the following syntax.

if *UNIX-command*

then

command

else

commands

fi

The `else' clause is, of course, optional. As noted before, the first UNIX command could be *anything*, since every command has a return code. The result is TRUE if it evaluates to *zero* and false otherwise (in contrast to the conventions in most languages). Multiple tests can be made using

if *UNIX-command*

then

commands

elif *UNIX-command*

then

commands

elif *UNIX-command*

then

commands

else

commands

fi

where `elif' means `else-if'.

The equivalent of the C-school's `switch' statement is a more Pascal-like `case' structure.

case *UNIX-command-or-variable* in

wildcard1) *commands* ;;

wildcard2) *commands* ;;

wildcard3) *commands* ;;

esac

This structure uses the wildcards to match the output of the command or variable in the first line. The first pattern which matches gets executed.

Input from the user in Bash

In shell you can read the value of a variable using the `read' command, with syntax

read *variable*

This reads in a string from the keyboard and terminates on a newline character. Under the old Bourne shell another way to do this is to use the `input' command to access a particular logical device. The keyboard device in the current terminal is `/dev/tty', so that one writes

variable = `line < /dev/tty`

which fetches a single line from the user. The command line is however not available in most GNU/Linux distributions.

Here are some examples of these commands. First a program which asks yes or no...

```
#!/bin/bash

#

# Yes or no

#

echo "Please answer yes or no: "

read answer
```

```
case $answer in

 y* | Y* | j* | J* )  echo YES!! ;;

 n* | N* )          echo NO!! ;;

 *)                 echo "Can't you answer a simple question?"

esac

echo The end
```

Notice the use of pattern matching and the `|' `OR' symbol.

```
#!/bin/bash
#
# Kernel check
#

if test ! -f /vmUNIX         # Check that the kernel is there!
then
  echo "This is not BSD UNIX...hmmm"
  if [ -f /hp-ux ]
  then
    echo "It's a Hewlett Packard machine!"
  fi
elif [ -w /vmUNIX ]
then
  echo "HEY!! The kernel is writable my me!";
else
  echo "The kernel is write protected."
  echo "The system is safe from me today."
fi
```

Loops in Bash

The loop structures in Bash and in the Bourne shell have the following syntax.

while *UNIX-command*

```
do
 commands
done
```

The first command will most likely be a test but, as before, it could in principle be any UNIX command. The `until' loop, reminiscent of BCPL, carries out a task until its argument evaluates to TRUE.

```
until UNIX-command
do
  commands
done
```

Finally the `for' structure has already been used above.

```
for variable in list
do
 commands
done
```

Often we want to be able to use an array of values as the list which for parses, but Bourne shell has no array variables. This problem is usually solved by making a long string separated by, for example, colons. For example, the $PATH variable has the form

```
PATH = /usr/bin:/bin:/local/gnu/bin
```

Bourne shell allows us to split such a string on whatever character we wish. Normally the split is made on spaces, but the variable `IFS' can be defined with a replacement. To make a loop over all directories in the command path we would therefore write

```
IFS=:

for name in $PATH; do

 commands

done
```

The best way to gain experience with these commands is through some examples.

```
#!/bin/bash
#
# Get text from user repeatedly
#
echo "Type away..."
```

```
while read TEXT
do

  echo You typed $TEXT

  if [ “$TEXT” = “quit” ]; then
    echo “(So I quit!)”
    exit 0
  fi
done

echo “HELP!”
```

This very simple script is a typical use for a while-loop. It gets text repeatedly until the user type `quit’. Since read never returns `false’ unless an error occurs or it detects an EOF (end of file) character CTRL-D, it will never exit without some help from an `if’ test. If it does receive a CTRL-D signal, the script prints `HELP!’.

```
#!/bin/bash
#
# Watch in the background for a particular user
# and give alarm if he/she logs in
#
# To be run in the background, using &
#

if [ $# -ne 1 ]; then
 echo “Give the name of the user as an argument” > /dev/tty
 exit 1
fi

echo “Looking for $1”

until users | grep -s $1
do
  sleep 60
done
```

```
echo "!!! WAKE UP !!!" > /dev/tty
echo "User $1 just logged in" > /dev/tty
```

This script uses `grep' in `silent mode' (-s option). i.e. grep never writes anything to the terminal. The only thing we are interested in is the return code the piped command produces. If `grep' detects a line containing the username we are interested in, then the result evaluates to TRUE and the sleep-loop exits.

Our final example is the kind of script which is useful for a system administrator. It transfers over the Network Information Service database files so that a slave server is up to date. All we have to do is make a list of the files and place it in a `for' loop. The names used below are the actual names of the NIS maps, well known to system administrators.

```
#!/bin/bash
#
# Update the NIS database maps on a client server. This program
# shouldn't have to be run, but sometimes things go wrong and we
# have to force a download from the main sever.

#
    PATH=/etc/yp:/usr/etc/yp:$PATH
    MASTER=myNISserver
for map in auto.direct auto.master ethers.byaddr ethers.byname\
      group.bygid group.byname hosts.byaddr hosts.byname\
      mail.aliases netgroup.byhost netgroup.byuser netgroup\
      netid.byname networks.byaddr networks.byname passwd.byname\
      passwd.byuid priss.byname protocols.byname protocols.bynumber\
      rpc.bynumber services.byname services usenetgroups.byname;
do
 ypxfr $1 -h $MASTER $map
done
```

Procedures and traps

One of the worthy features of the Bourne shell is that it allows you to define *subroutines* or *procedures*. Subroutines work just like subroutines in any other programming language. They are executed in same shell (not as a sub-process).

Here is an interesting program which demonstrates two useful things at the same time. First of all, it shows how to make a hierarchical subroutine structure using the Bourne shell. Secondly, it shows how the`trap' directive can be used to trap signals, so that Bourne shell programs can exit safely when they are killed or when CTRL-C is typed.

```
#!/bin/bash
```

```
#
#  How to make a signal handler in Bourne Shell
#  using subroutines
#

#####################################################
# Level 2
#####################################################

ReallyQuit()
{
while true
do
  echo "Do you really want to quit?"
  read answer

  case $answer in

     y* | Y* ) return 0;;
     *)       echo "Resuming..."
              return 1;;

  esac

done
}

#####################################################
# Level 1
#####################################################

SignalHandler()

{
if ReallyQuit          # Call a function
```

```
then
  exit 0
else
  return 0
fi
}

#########################################################
# Level 0 : main program
#########################################################

trap SignalHandler 2 15  # Trap kill signals 2 and 15

echo "Type some lines of text..."

while read text
do

  echo "$text - CTRL-C to exit"

done
```

Note that the logical tree structure of this program is upside down (the highest level comes at the bottom). This is because all subroutines must be defined before they are used.

This example concludes our survey of Bash and the Bourne shell.

setuid and setgid scripts

The superuser `root' is the only privileged user in UNIX. All other users have only restricted access to the system. Usually this is desirable, but sometimes it is a nuisance.

A setuid script is a script which has its *setuid-bit* set. When such a script is executed by a user, it is run with all the rights and privileges of the owner of the script. All of the commands in the script are executed as the owner of the file and not with the user-id of the person who ran the script. If the owner of the setuid script is `root' then the commands in the script are run with *root privileges*!

Setuid scripts are clearly a touchy security issue. When giving away one's rights to another user (especially those of `root') one is tempting hackers. Setuid scripts should be *avoided*.

A setgid program is almost the same, but only the group id is set to that of the owner of the file. Often the effect is the same.

An example of a setuid program is the `ps' program. `ps' lists all of the processes running in the kernel. In order to do this it needs permission to access the private data structures in the kernel. By making`ps' setgid root, it allows ordinary users to be able to read as much as the writers of `ps' thought fit, but no more.

Naturally, only the superuser can make a file setuid or setgid root.

Exercises

- Write an improved `which' command in Bash.
- Make a counter program which records in a file how many times you log in to your account. You can call this in your .bashrc file.
- Make a Bourne shell script to kill all the processes owned by a particular user. (Note, that if you are not the superuser, you cannot kill processes owned by other users.)
- Write a script to replace the `rm' command with something safer. Think about a way of implementing `rm' so that it is possible to get deleted files back again in case of emergencies. This is not possible using the normal `rm' command. Hint: save files in a hidden directory `.deleted'. Make your script delete files in the `. deleted' directory if they are older than a week, so that you don't fill up the disk with rubbish.
- Suppose you have a bunch of files with a particular file-extension: write a script in Bash to change the extension to something else. e.g. to change *.C into *.c. Give the old and new extensions as arguments to the script.
- Write a program in Bash to search for files in the current directory which contain a certain string. e.g. search for all files which contain the word "if". Hint: use the "find" command.
- Use the manual pages to find out about the commands `at', `batch' and `atq'. Test these commands by executing the shell command `date' at some time of your choice. Use the `-m' option so that the result of the job is mailed to you.
- Write a script in Bash to list all of the files bigger than a certain size starting from the current directory, and including all subdirectories. This kind of program is useful for system administrators when a disk becomes full.

C SHELL

Programmers who are used to C or C++ often find it easier to program in C-shell because there are strong similarities between the two.

.cshrc and .login files

Most users run the C-shell `/bin/csh' as their login environment, or these days, preferably the `tcsh' which is an improved version of csh. When a user logs in to a UNIX system the C-shell starts by reading some files which configure the environment by defining variables like path.

- The file `.cshrc' is searched for in your home directory. i.e. `~/.cshrc'. If it is found, its contents are interpreted by the C-shell as C-shell instructions, before giving you the command prompt(5).
- If and only if this is the *login shell* (not a sub-shell that you have started after login) then the file `~/.login' is searched for and executed.

With the advent of the X11 windowing system, this has changed slightly. Since the window system takes over the entire login procedure, users never get to run `login shells›, since the login shell is used up by the X11 system. On an X-terminal or host running X the `.login› file normally has no effect.

With some thought, the `.login› file can be eliminated entirely, and we can put everything into the .cshrc file. Here is a very simple example `.cshrc› file.

```
#
# .cshrc - read in by every csh that starts.
#

# Set the default file creation mask
umask 077

# Set the path
set path=( /usr/local/bin /usr/bin/X11 /usr/ucb /bin /usr/bin . )

# Exit here if the shell is not interactive
if ( $?prompt == 0 ) exit

# Set some variables

set noclobber notify filec nobeep
set history=100
set prompt=»`hostname`%»
set prompt2 = «%m %h>»    # tcsh, prompt for foreach and while

setenv PRINTER myprinter
setenv LD_LIBRARY_PATH /usr/lib:/usr/local/lib:/usr/openwin/lib
```

Aliases are shortcuts to UNIX commands

alias passwd yppasswd

alias dir ‹ls -lg \!* | more›

alias sys ‹ps aux | more›

alias h history

It is possible to make a much more complicated .cshrc file than this. The advent of distributed computing and NFS (Network file system) means that you might log into many different machines running different versions of UNIX. The command path would have to be set differently for each type of machine.

Defining variables with set, setenv

We have already seen in the examples above how to define variables in C-shell. Let's formalize this. To define a local variable -- that is, one which will not get passed on to programs and sub-shells running under the current shell, we write

set local = “some string”

set myname = “`whoami`”

These variables are then referred to by using the dollar `$' symbol. i.e. The value of the variable `local' is `$local'.

echo $local $myname

Global variables, that is variables which all sub-shells inherit from the current shell are defined using `setenv'

setenv GLOBAL “Some other string”

setenv MYNAME “`who am i`”

Their values are also referred to using the `$' symbol. Notice that set uses an `=' sign while `setenv' does not.

Variables can be also created without a value. The shell uses this method to switch on and off certain features, using variables like `noclobber' and `noglob'. For instance

nexus% set flag

nexus% if ($?flag) echo ‘Flag is set!’

Flag is set!

nexus% unset flag

nexus% if ($?flag) echo ‘Flag is set!’

nexus%

The operator `$?*variable*' is `true' if *variable* exists and `false' if it does not. It does not matter whether the variable holds any information.

The commands `unset› and `unsetenv› can be used to undefine or delete variables when you don›t want them anymore.

Arrays

A useful facility in the C-shell is the ability to make arrays out of strings and other variables. The round parentheses `(..)' do this. For example, look at the following commands.

nexus% set array = (a b c d)

nexus% echo $array[1]

a

nexus% echo $array[2]

b

nexus% echo $array[$#array]

d

nexus% set noarray = ("a b c d")

nexus% echo $noarray[1]

a b c d

nexus% echo $noarray[$#noarray]

a b c d

The first command defines an array containing the elements `a b c d'. The elements of the array are referred to using square brackets `[..]' and the first element is `$array[1]'. The last element is`$array[4]'. *NOTE: this is not the same as in C or C++ where the first element of the array is the zeroth element!*

The special operator `$#' returns the number of elements in an array. This gives us a simple way of finding the end of the array. For example

nexus% echo $#path

23

nexus% echo "The last element in path is $path[$#path]"

The last element in path is .

To find the next last element we need to be able to do arithmetic. We'll come back to this later.

Pipes and redirection in csh

The symbols

< > >> << | &

have a special meaning in the shell. By default, most commands take their input from the file `stdin' (the keyboard) and write their output to the file `stdout' and their error messages to the file `stderr'(normally, both of these output files are defined to be the current terminal device `/dev/tty', or `/dev/console').

`stdin', `stdout' and `stderr', known collectively as `stdio', can be redefined or *redirected* so that information is taken from or sent to a different file. The output direction can be changed with the symbol`>'. For example,

echo testing > myfile

produces a file called `myfile› which contains the string `testing›. The single `>› (greater than) sign always creates a new file, whereas the double `>>› appends to the end of a file, if it already exists. So the first of the commands

echo blah blah >> myfile

echo Newfile > myfile

adds a second line to `myfile› after `testing›, whereas the second command writes over `myfile› and ends up with just one line `Newfile›.

Now suppose we mistype a command

ehco test > myfile

The command `ehco› does not exist and so the error message `ehco: Command not found› appears on the terminal. This error message was sent to *stderr* -- so even though we redirected output to a file, the error message appeared on the screen to tell us that an error occurred. Even this can be changed. `stderr' can also be redirected by adding an ampersand `&' character to the `>' symbol. The command

ehco test >& myfile

results in the file `myfile› being created, containing the error message `ehco: Command not found›.

The input direction can be changed using the `<› symbol for example

/bin/mail mark < message

would send the file `message› to the user `mark› by electronic mail. The mail program takes its input from the file instead of waiting for keyboard input.

There are some refinements to the redirection symbols. First of all, let us introduce the C-shell variable `noclobber›. If this variable is set with a command like

set noclobber

then files will not be overwritten by the `>› command. If one tries to redirect output to an existing file, the following happens.

UNIX% set noclobber

UNIX% touch blah # create an empty file blah

UNIX% echo test > blah

blah: File exists.

If you are nervous about overwriting files, then you can set `noclobber› in your `. cshrc› file. `noclobber› can be overridden using the pling `!› symbol. So

UNIX% set noclobber

UNIX% touch blah # create an empty file blah

UNIX% echo test >! blah

writes over the file `blah› even though `noclobber› is set.

Here are some other combinations of redirection symbols

`>>›

Append, including `stderr›

`>>!›

Append, ignoring `noclobber›

`>>&!›

Append `stdout›, `stderr›, ignore `noclobber›

`<<›

See below.

The last of these commands reads from the standard input until it finds a line which contains a word. It then feeds all of this input into the program concerned. For example,

nexus% mail mark <<quit

nexus 1> Hello mark

nexus 2> Nothing much to say...

nexus 2> so bye

nexus 2>

nexus 2> quit

Sending mail...

Mail sent!

The mail message contains all the lines up to, but not including `marker›. This method can also be used to print text verbatim from a file without using multiple echo commands. Inside a script one may write:

```
cat << «marker»;

        MENU


   1) choice 1
   2) choice 2
   ...

marker
```

The cat command writes directly to stdout and the input is redirected and taken directly from the script file.

A very useful construction is the `pipe› facility. Using the `|› symbol one can feed the `stdout› of one program straight into the `stdin› of another program. Similarly with `|&› both `stdout› and `stderr›can be piped into the input of another program. This is very convenient. For instance, look up the following commands in the manual and try them.

ps aux | more

echo ‹Keep on sharpening them there knives!› | mail henry

vmstat 1 | head

ls -l /etc | tail

Note that when piping both standard input and standard error to another program, the two files *do not mix synchronously*. Often `stderr' appears first.

`tee' and `script'

Occasionally you might want to have a copy of what you see on your terminal sent to a file. `tee' and `script' do this. For instance,

find / -type l -print | tee myfile

sends a copy of the output of `find' to the file `myfile'. `tee' can split the output into as many files as you want:

command | tee *file1 file2* ....

You can also choose to record the output an entire shell session using the `script' command.

nexus% script mysession

Script started, file is mysession

nexus% echo Big brother is scripting you

Big brother is scripting you

nexus% exit

exit

Script done, file is mysession

The file `mysession' is a text file which contains a transcript of the session.

Scripts with arguments

One of the useful features of the shell is that you can use the normal UNIX commands to make programs called *scripts*. To make a script, you just create a file containing shell commands you want to execute and make sure that the first line of the file looks like the following example.

#!/bin/csh -f

#

A simple script: check for user's mail

```
#
#

set path = ( /bin /usr/ucb )            # Set the local path

cd /var/spool/mail                     # Change dir

foreach uid ( * )

  echo "$uid has mail in the intray! "   # space prevents an error!

end
```

The sequence `#!/bin/csh' means that the following commands are to be fed into `/bin/csh'. The two symbols `#!' must be the very first two characters in the file. The `-f' option means that your `.cshrc'file is not read by the shell when it starts up. The file containing this script must be executable (see `chmod') and must be in the current path, like all other programs.

Like C programs, C-shell scripts can accept command line arguments. Suppose you want to make a program to say hello to some other users who are logged onto the system.

```
say-hello mark sarah mel
```

To do this you need to know the names that were typed on the command line. These names are copied into an array in the C-shell called the *argument vector*, or `argv'. To read these arguments, you just treat`argv' as an array.

```
#!/bin/csh -f
#
# Say hello
#

foreach name ( $argv )

  echo Saying hello to $name
  echo "Hello from $user! " | write $name

end
```

The elements of the array can be referred to as `argv[1]'..`argv[$#argv]' as usual. They can also be referred to as `$1'..`$3' up to the last acceptable number. This makes

C-shell compatible with the Bourne shell as far as arguments are concerned. One extra flourish in this method is that you can also refer to the name of the program itself as `$0'. For example,

```
#!/bin/csh -f

echo This is program $0 running for $user
```

`$argv' represents all the arguments. You can also use `$*' from the Bourne shell.

Sub-shells ()

The C-shell does not allow you to define subroutines or functions, but you can create a local shell, with its own private variables by enclosing commands in parentheses.

```
#!/bin/csh


cd /etc


( cd /usr/bin; ls * ) > myfile


pwd
```

This program changes the working directory to /etc and then executes a subshell which *inside the brackets* changes directory to /usr/bin and lists the files there. The output of this private shell are sent to a file `myfile'. At the end we print out the current working directory just to show that the `cd' command in brackets had no effect on the main program.

Normally both parentheses must be on the same line. If a subshell command line gets too long, so that the brackets are not on the same line, you have to use backslash characters to continue the lines,

```
 ( command \
   command \
   command \
)
```

Tests and conditions

No programming language would be complete without tests and loops. C-shell has two kinds of decision structure: the `if..then..else' and the `switch' structure. These are closely related to their C counterparts. The syntax of these is

if (*condition*) *command*

if (*condition*) then

  command

  command..

```
else
  command
  command..
endif


switch (string)

 case one:
        commands
        breaksw

 case two:
        commands
        breaksw

 ...

endsw
```

In the latter case, no commands should appear on the same line as a `case' statement, or they will be ignored. Also, if the `breaksw' commands are omitted, then control flows through all the commands for case 2, case 3 etc, exactly as it does in the C programming language.

We shall consider some examples of these statements in a moment, but first it is worth listing some important tests which can be used in `if' questions to find out information about files.

`-r *file*'

True if the file exists and is readable

`-w *file*'

True if the file exists and is writable

`-x *file*'

True if the file exists and is executable

`-e *file*'

True if the file simply exists

`-z *file*'

True if the file exists and is empty

`-f *file*’

True if the file is a plain file

`-d *file*’

True if the file is a directory

We shall also have need of the following comparison operators.

`==’

is equal to (string comparison)

`!=’

is not equal to

`>’

is greater than

`<’

is less than

`>=’

is greater than or equal to

`<=’

is less than or equal to

`=~’

matches a wildcard

`!~’

does not match a wildcard

The simplest way to learn about these statements is to use them, so we shall now look at some examples.

```
#!/bin/csh -f
#
#  Safe copy from <arg[1]> to <arg[2]>
#
#

if ($#argv != 2) then

  echo “Syntax: copy <from-file> <to-file>”
  exit 0
```

```
endif

if ( -f $argv[2] ) then

  echo "File exists. Copy anyway?"

  switch ( $< )                # Get a line from user

    case y:
          breaksw

    default:
          echo "Doing nothing!"
          exit 0

  endsw

endif

echo -n "Copying $argv[1] to $argv[2]..."
cp $argv[1] $argv[2]
echo done

endif
```

This script tries to copy a file from one location to another. If the user does not type exactly two arguments, the script quits with a message about the correct syntax. Otherwise it tests to see whether a plain file has the same name as the file the user wanted to copy to. If such a file exists, it asks the user if he/she wants to continue before proceeding to copy.

Switch example: configure script

Here is another example which compiles a software package. This is a problem we shall return to later See section Make. The problem this script tries to address is the following. There are many different versions of UNIX and they are not exactly compatible with one another. The program this file compiles has to work on any kind of UNIX, so it tries first to determine what kind of UNIX system the script is being run on by calling `uname'. Then it defines a variable `MAKE' which contains the path to the `make' program which will build *software*. The make program reads a file called `Makefile' which contains instructions for compiling the program, but this file needs to know the type of UNIX, so the script first copies a file `Makefile.src' using `sed' replace a dummy string with the real name of the UNIX. Then it calls make and sets the correct permission on the file using `chmod'.

```
#!/bin/csh -f
#####################################################
#
#
# CONFIGURE Makefile AND BUILD software
#
#
#####################################################

set NAME = ( `uname -r -s` )

switch ($NAME[1])

  case SunOS*:
        switch ($NAME[2])

          case 4*:
                setenv TYPE SUN4
                setenv MAKE /bin/make
                breaksw
          case 5*:
                setenv TYPE SOLARIS
                setenv MAKE /usr/ccs/bin/make
                breaksw

        endsw
        breaksw

  case ULTRIX*:
        setenv TYPE ULTRIX
        setenv MAKE /bin/make
```

```
            breaksw
    case HP-UX*:
            setenv TYPE HPUX
            setenv MAKE /bin/make
            breaksw
    case AIX*:
            setenv TYPE AIX
            setenv MAKE /bin/make
            breaksw

    case OSF*:
            setenv TYPE OSF
            setenv MAKE /bin/make
            breaksw
    case IRIX*:
            setenv TYPE IRIX
            setenv MAKE /bin/make
            breaksw

    default:
            echo Unknown architecture $NAME[1]

endsw

# Generate Makefile from source file

sed s/HOSTTYPE/$TYPE/ Makefile.src > Makefile

echo "Making software. Type CTRL-C to abort and edit Makefile"

$MAKE software          # call make to build program
chmod 755 software      # set correct protection
```

Loops in csh

The C-shell has three loop structures: `repeat', `while' and `foreach'. We have already seen some examples of the `foreach' loop.

The structure of these loops is as follows

repeat *number-of-times command*

while (*test expression*)

commands

end

foreach *control-variable* (*list-or-array*)

commands

end

The commands `break' and `continue' can be used to break out of the loops at any time. Here are some examples.

repeat 2 echo "Yo!" | write mark

This sends the message "Yo!" to mark's terminal twice.

repeat 5 echo `echo "Shutdown time! Log out now" | wall ; sleep 30` ; halt

This example repeats the command `echo Shutdown time...' five times at 30 second intervals, before shutting down the system. Only the superuser can run this command! Note the strange construction with `echo echo'. This is to force the repeat command to take two shell commands as an argument. (Try to explain why this works for yourself.)

Input from the user

```
# Test a user response

echo "Answer y/n (yes or no)"

set valid = false

while ( $valid == false )

  switch ( $< )
```

```
    case y:
        echo "You answered yes"
        set valid = true
        breaksw

    case n:
        echo "You answered no"
        set valid = true
        breaksw

    default:
        echo "Invalid response, try again"
        breaksw

  endsw

end
```

Notice that it would have been simpler to replace the two lines

```
set valid = true
breaksw
```

by a single line `break'. `breaksw' jumps out of the switch construction, after which the `while' test fails. `break' jumps out of the entire while loop.

Extracting parts of a pathname

A path name consists of a number of different parts:

- The path to the directory where a file is held.
- The name of the file itself.
- The file extension (after a dot).

By using one of the following modifiers, we can extract these different elements.

`:h'

The path to the file

`:t'

The filename itself

`:e'

The file extension

`:r'

The complete file-path minus the file extension

Here are some examples and the results:

```
set f = ~/progs/c++/test.C

echo $f:h

 /home/mark/progs/c++

echo $f:t

  test.C

echo $f:e

   C
echo $f:r
   /home/mark/progs/c++/test
```

Arithmetic

Before using these features in a real script, we need one more possibility: numerical addition, subtraction and multiplication etc.

To tell the C-shell that you want to perform an operation on numbers rather than strings, you use the `@' symbol followed by a space. Then the following operations are possible.

```
@ var = 45              # Assign a numerical value to var
echo $var               # Print the value

@ var = $var + 34       # Add 34 to var
@ var += 34             # Add 34 to var

@ var -= 1              # subtract 1 from var
@ var *= 5              # Multiply var by 5
```

```
@ var /= 3                # Divide var by 3 (integer division)
@ var %= 3                # Remainder after dividing var by 3

@ var++                   # Increment var by 1
@ var--                   # Decrement var by 1

@ array[1] = 5            # Numerical array

@ logic = ( $x > 6 && $x < 10)  # AND
@ logic = ( $x > 6 || $x < 10)  # OR
@ false = ! $var          # Logical NOT

@ bits = ( $x | $y )      # Bitwise OR
@ bits = ( $x ^ $y )      # Bitwise XOR
@ bits = ( $x & $y )      # Bitwise AND

@ shifted = ( $var >> 2 )    # Bitwise shift right
@ back    = ( $var << 2 )    # Bitwise shift left
```

These operators are precisely those found in the C programming language.

Examples

The following script uses the operators in the last two sections to take a list of files with a given file extension (say `.doc') and change it for another (say `.tex'). This is a partial solution to the limitation of not being able to do multiple renames in shell.

```
#!/bin/csh -f
###############################################################
#
# Change file extension for multiple files
#
###############################################################

if ($#argv < 2) then
  echo Syntax: chext oldpattern newextension
  echo "e.g: chext *.doc tex "
  exit 0
```

```
endif

mkdir /tmp/chext.$user              # Make a scratch area

set newext="$argv[$#argv]"          # Last arg is new ext
set oldext="$argv[1]:e"

echo "Old extension was ($oldext)""
echo "New extension ($newext) -- okay? (y/n)"

switch( $< )

  case y:
        breaksw
  default:
        echo "Nothing done."
        exit 0
endsw

###################################################################
# Remove the last file extension from files
###################################################################

 i = 0

foreach file ($argv)
  i++
 if ( $i == $#argv ) break
 cp $file /tmp/chext.$user/$file:r      # temporary store

end

###################################################################
# Add .newext file extension to files
###################################################################
```

```
set array = (`ls /tmp/chext.$user`)

foreach file ($array)

 if ( -f $file.$newext ) then
  echo  destination file $file.$newext exists. No action taken.
  continue
 endif

 cp /tmp/chext.$user/$file $file.$newext
 rm $file.$oldext

end

rm -r /tmp/chext.$user
```

Here is another example to try to decipher. Use the manual pages to find out about `awk'. This script can be written much more easily in Perl or C, as we shall see in the next chapters. It is also trivially implemented as a script in the system administration language cfengine.

```
#!/bin/csh -f
#################################################################
#
# KILL all processes owned by $argv[1] with PID > $argv[2]
#
#################################################################

if ("`whoami`" != "root") then
 echo Permission denied
 exit 0
endif

if ( $#argv < 1 || $#argv > 2 ) then
 echo Usage: KILL username lowest-pid
 exit 0
endif
```

```
if ( $argv[1] == "root") then
  echo No! Too dangerous -- system will crash
  exit 0
endif

#################################################################
# Kill everything
#################################################################

if ( $#argv == 1 ) then

  set killarray = ( `ps aux |  awk '{ if ($1 == user) \
{printf "%s ",$2}}' user=$argv[1]` )

  foreach process ($killarray)

    kill -1 $process
    kill -15 $process > /dev/null
    kill -9 $process > /dev/null

    if ("`kill -9 $process | egrep -e 'No such process'`" == "") then
      echo "Warning - $process would not die - try again"
    endif
  end

#################################################################
# Start from a certain PID
#################################################################

else if ( $#argv == 2 ) then

  set killarray = ( `ps aux |  awk '{ if ($1 == user && $2 > uid) \
{printf "%s ",$2}}' user=$argv[1] uid=$argv[2]` )
```

```
foreach process ($killarray)

   kill -1 $process > /dev/null
   kill -15 $process
   sleep 2
   kill -9 $process > /dev/null

   if ("`kill -9 $process | egrep -e 'No such process'`" == "") then
     echo "Warning - $process would not die - try again"
   endif
end

endif
```

This program would be better written in C or Perl.

Summary: Limitations of shell programming

To summarize the last two long and oppressive chapters we shall take a step back from the details and look at what we have achieved.

The idea behind the shell is to provide a user interface, with access to the system's facilities at a simple level. In the 70's user interfaces were not designed to be user-friendly. The UNIX shell is not particularly use friendly, but it is very powerful. Perhaps it would have been enough to provide only commands to allow users to write C programs. Since all of the system functions are available from C, that would certainly allow everyone to do what anything that UNIX can do. But shell programming is much more *immediate* than C. It is an environment of *frequently used tools*. Also for quick programming solutions: C is a compiled language, whereas the shell is an interpreter. A quick shell program can solve many problems in no time at all, without having to compile anything.

Shell programming is only useful for `quick and easy' programs. To use it for anything serious is an abuse. Programming difficult things in shell is clumsy, and it is difficult to get returned-information (like error messages) back in a useful form. Besides, shell scripts are slow compared to real programs since they involve starting a new program for each new command.

These difficulties are solved partly by Perl, which we shall consider next -- but in the final analysis, real programs of substance need to be written in C. Contrary to popular belief, this is not more difficult than programming in the shell -- in fact, many things are much simpler, because all of the shell commands originated as C functions. The shell is an extra layer of the UNIX onion which we have to battle our way through to get where we're going.

SECTION III: INTERMEDIARY TOPICS IN UNIX PROGRAMMING

3
CHAPTER

INTERMEDIARY TOPICS IN UNIX PROGRAMMING

Mark Burgess

A NOTE ABOUT UNIX SYSTEM CALLS AND STANDARDS

Most of the system calls in UNIX return data in the form of `struct' variables. Sometimes these are structures used by the operating system itself -- in other cases they are just put together so that programmers can handle a packet of data in a convenient way.

If in doubt, you can find the definitions of these structures in the relevant include files under `/usr/include'.

Since UNIX comes in many flavours the system calls are not always compatible and may have different options and arguments. Because of this there is a number of standardizing organizations for UNIX. One of them is POSIX which is an organization run by the major UNIX vendors. Programs written for UNIX are now expected to be POSIX compliant. This is not something you need to think about at the level of this course, but you should certainly remember that there exist programming standards and that these should be adhered to. The aim is to work towards a single standard UNIX.

COMPILING: `CC', `LD' AND `A.OUT'

The C compiler on the UNIX system is traditionally called `cc' and has always been a traditional part of every UNIX environment. Recently several UNIX vendors have stopped including the C compiler as a part of their operating systems and instead sell a compiler separately. Fortunately there is a public domain Free Software version of the compiler called `gcc' (the GNU C compiler). We shall use this in all the examples.

To compile a program consisting of several files of code, we first compile all of the separate pieces without trying to link them. There are therefore two stages: first we

---

Citation: Mark Burgess, Intermediary Topics in UNIX programming, http://www.iu.hio.no/~mark/unix/unix.html.

turn `.c' files into `.o' files. This compiles code but does not fix any address references. Then we link all `.o' files into the final executable, including any libraries which are used.

Let's suppose we have files `a.c', `b.c' and `c.c'. We write:

```
gcc -c a.c b.c c.c
```

This creates files `a.o', `b.o' and `c.o'. Next we link them into one file called `myprog'.

```
gcc -o myprog  a.o b.o c.o
```

If the naming option `-o myprog' is not used, the link `ld' uses the default name *a. out* for the executable file.

Libraries and `LD_LIBRARY_PATH›

The resulting file is called `myprog' and includes references only to the standard library `libc'. If we wish to link in the math library `libm' or the cursor movement library `libcurses' -- or in general, a library called `libBLAH' , we need to use the `-l' directive.

```
gcc -o myprog files.o  -lm -lcurses -lBLAH
```

The compiler looks for a suitable library in all of the directories listed in the environment variable `LD_LIBRARY_PATH›. Alternatively we can add a directory to the search path by using the `-L›. option:

```
gcc -o myprog files.o -L/usr/local/lib -lm -lcurses -lBLAH
```

Include files

Normally the compiler looks for include files only in the directory `/usr/include'. We can add further paths to search using the `-I' option.

```
gcc -o myprog file.c  -I/usr/local/include -I/usr/local/X11/include
```

Previously, UNIX libraries have been in `a.out' code format, but recent releases of UNIX have gone over to a more efficient and flexible format called ELF (executable and linking format).

Shared and static libraries

Libraries are collections of C functions which the operating system creators have written for our convenience. The source code for such a library is just the source for a collection of functions -- there is nomain program.

There are two kinds of library used by modern operating systems: *archive libraries* or static libraries and shared libraries or dynamical libraries. An archive library has a name of the form

lib*name*.a

When an archive library is linked to a program, it is appended lock, stock and barrel to the program code. This uses a lot of disk space and makes the size of the compiled program very large. Shared libraries (shared objects `so' or shared archives `sa' generally have names of the form)

lib*name*.so

lib*name*.sa

often with version numbers appended. When a program is linked with a shared library the code is not appended to the program. Instead pointers to the shared objects are created and the library is loaded at runtime, thus avoiding the problem of having to store the library effectively multiple times on the disk.

To make an archive library we compile all of the functions we wish to include in the library

```
gcc -c function1.c function2.c ...
```

and then join the files using the `ar' command.

```
ar rcv libMYLIB.a function1.o
ar rcv libMYLIB.a function2.o
```

To make a shared library one provides an option to the linker program. The exact method is different in different operating systems, so you should look at the manual page for ld on your system. Under SunOS 4 we take the object files `*.o' and run

```
ld -o libMYLIB.so.1.1 -assert pure-text *.o
```

Under HPUX, we write

```
ld -b -o libMYLIB.so.1.1 *.o
```

With the GNU linker, you write

```
ld -shared -o libMYLIB.so.1.1 *.o
```

NOTE: when you add a shared library to the system under SunOS or GNU/Linux you must run the command `ldconfig', making sure that the path to the library is included in `LD_LIBRARY_PATH'. SunOS and GNU/Linux use a cache file `/etc/ld.so.cache' to keep current versions of libraries. GNU/Linux also uses a configuration file called `/etc/ld.so.conf'.

Knowing about important paths: directory structure

It is important to understand how the C compiler finds the files it needs. We have already mentioned the `-I' and `-L' options to the compilation command line. In general, all system include files can be found in the directory `/usr/include' and subdirectories of this directory. All system libraries can be found in `/usr/lib'.

Many packages build their own libraries and keep the relevant files in separate directories so that if the system gets reinstalled, they do not get deleted. This is true for example of the X-windows system. The include and library files for this are typically kept in directories which look something like `/usr/local/X11R5/include' and `/usr/X11R6/lib'. That means that we need to give all of this information to the compiler. Compiling a program becomes a complicated task in many cases so we need some kind of script to help us perform the task. The UNIX tool make was designed for this purpose.

MAKE

Nowadays compilers are often sold with fancy user environments driven by menus which make it easier to compile programs. UNIX has similar environments but all of them use shell-based command line compilation beneath the surface. That is because UNIX programmers are used to writing large and complex programs which occupy many directories and subdirectories. Each directory has to be adapted or configured to fit the particular flavour of UNIX system it is being compiled upon. Interactive user environments are very poor at performing this kind of service. UNIX solves the problem of compiling enormous *trees* of software (such as the UNIX system itself!) by using a compilation language called `make'. Such language files can be generated automatically by scripts, allowing very complex programs to configure and compile themselves from a single control script.

Compiling large projects

Typing lines like

```
cc -c file1.c file2.c ...
cc -o target file1.o ....
```

repeatedly to compile a complicated program can be a real nuisance. One possibility would therefore be to keep all the commands in a script. This could waste a lot of time though. Suppose you are working on a big project which consists of many lines of source code -- but are editing only one file. You really only want to recompile the file you are working on and then relink the resulting object file with all of the other object files. Recompiling the other files which hadn't changed would be a waste of time. But that would mean that you would have to change the script each time you change what you need to compile.

A better solution is to use the `make' command. `make' was designed for precisely this purpose. To use `make', we create a file called `Makefile' in the same directory as our program. `make' is a quite general program for building software. It is not specifically tied to the C programming language--- it can be used in any programming language.

A `make' configuration file, called a `Makefile', contains rules which describe how to compile or build all of the pieces of a program. For example, even without telling it specifically, make knows that in order to go from `prog.c' to `prog.o' the command `cc -c prog.c' must be executed. A Makefile works by making such associations. The Makefile contains a list of all of the files which compose the program and rules as to how to get to the finished product from the source.

The idea is that, to compile a program, we just have to type make. `make' then reads the Makefile and compiles all of the parts which need compiling. It does not recompile files which have not changed since the last compilation! How does it do this? `make' works by comparing the time-stamp on the file it needs to create with the time-stamp on the file which is to be compiled. If the compiled version exists and is newer than its source then the source does not need to be recompiled.

To make this idea work in practice, `make' has to know how to go through the steps of compiling a program. Some default rules are defined in a global configuration file, e.g.

/usr/include/make/default.mk

Let's consider an example of what happens for the the three files `a.c', `b.c' and `c.c' in the example above -- and let's not worry about what the Makefile looks like yet.

The first time we compile, only the `.c' files exist. When we type `make', the program looks at its rules and finds that it has to make a file called `myprog'. To make this it needs to execute the command

```
gcc -o myprog  a.o b.o c.o
```

So it looks for `a.o' etc and doesn't find them. It now goes to a kind of subroutine and looks to see if it has any rules for making files called `.o' and it discovers that these are made by compiling with the `gcc -c' option. Since the files do not exist, it does this. Now the files `a.o b.o c.o' exist and it jumps back to the original problem of trying to make `myprog'. All the files it needs now exist and so it executes the command and builds `myprog'.

If we now edit `a.c', and type `make' once again -- it goes through the same procedure as before but now it finds all of the files. So it compares the dates on the files -- if the source is newer than the result, it recompiles.

By using this recursive method, `make' only compiles those parts of a program which need compiling.

Makefiles

To write a Makefile, we have to tell `make' about *dependencies*. The dependencies of a file are all of those files which are required to build it. Thus, the dependencies of `myprog' are `a.o', `b.o' and `c.o'. The dependencies of `a.o' are simply `a.c', the dependencies of `b.o' are `b.c' and so on.

A Makefile consists of rules of the form:

```
target : dependencies
TAB            rule;
```

The target is the thing we want to build, the dependencies are like subroutines to be executed first if they do not exist. Finally the rule is to be executed if all if the dependencies exist; it takes the dependencies and turns them into the target. There are two important things to remember:

- The file names must start on the first character of a line.
- There must be a TAB character at the beginning of every rule or action. If there are spaces instead of tabs, or no tab at all, `make' will signal an error. This bizarre feature can cause a lot of confusion.

Let's look at an example Makefile for a program which consists of two course files `main.c' and `other.c' and which makes use of a library called `libdb' which lies in the directory `/usr/local/lib'. Our aim is to build a program called database:

```
#
# Simple Makefile for `database'
#

# First define a macro

OBJ = main.o other.o

CC = gcc
CFLAGS = -I/usr/local/include
LDFLAGS = -L/usr/local/lib -ldb
INSTALLDIR = /usr/local/bin
#
# Rules start here. Note that the $@ variable becomes the name of the
# executable file. In this case it is taken from the ${OBJ} variable
#

database: ${OBJ}
	${CC} -o $@ ${OBJ} ${LDFLAGS}

#
# If a header file changes, normally we need to recompile everything.
# There is no way that make can know this unless we write a rule which
# forces it to rebuild all .o files if the header file changes...
#

${OBJ}: ${HEADERS}

#
```

```
# As well as special rules for special files we can also define a
# “suffix rule”. This is a rule which tells us how to build all files
# of a certain type. Here is a rule to get .o files from .c files.
# The $< variable is like $? but is only used in suffix rules.
#

.c.o:
        ${CC} -c ${CFLAGS} $<

########################################################################
###
# Clean up
########################################################################
###

 #
 # Make can also perform ordinary shell command jobs
 # “make tidy” here performs a cleanup operation
 #

clean:
        rm -f ${OBJ}
        rm -f y.tab.c lex.yy.c y.tab.h
        rm -f y.tab lex.yy
        rm -f *% *~ *.o
        rm -f mconfig.tab.c mconfig.tab.h a.out
        rm -f man.dvi man.aux man.log man.toc
        rm -f cfengine.tar.gz cfengine.tar cfengine.tar.Z
        make tidy
        rm -f cfengine
```

install: ${INSTALLDIR}/database

    cp database ${INSTALLDIR}/database

The Makefile above can be invoked in several ways.

make

make database

make clean

make install

If we simple type `make' i.e. the first of these choices, `make' takes the first of the rules it finds as the object to build. In this case the rule is `database', so the first two forms above are equivalent.

On the other hand, if we type

make clean

then execution starts at the rule for `clean', which is normally used to remove all files except the original source code. Make `install' causes the compiled program to be installed at its intended destination.

`make' uses some special variables (which resemble the special variables used in Perl -- but don't confuse them). The most useful one is `$@' which represents the current *target* -- or the object which `make'would like to compile. i.e. as `make' checks each file it would like to compile, `$@' is set to the current filename.

$@

This evaluates to the current target i.e. the name of the object you are currently trying to build. It is normal to use this as the final name of the program when compiling

$?

This is used only outside of suffix rules and means the name of all the files which must be compiled in order to build the current target.

target: file1.o file2.o

TAB cc -o $@ $?

$<

This is only used in suffix rules. It has the same meaning as `$?› but only in suffix rules. It stands for the pre-requisite, or the file which must be compiled in order to make a given object.

Note that, because `make› has some default rules defined in its configuration file, a single-file C program can be compiled very easily by typing

make filename.c

This is equivalent to

cc -c filename.c

cc -o filename filename.o

New suffix rules for C++

Standard rules for C++ are not often built into UNIX systems at the time of writing, but we can create them in our own Makefiles very easily. Here we shall use the GNU compiler g++'s conventions for C++ files. Here is a sample Makefile for using C++. Note that the `.SUFFIXES' command must be used to declare new endings or file extensions.

```
######################################################################
#
# This is the Makefile for g++
#
######################################################################


OBJ = cpp-prog.o X.o Y.o Z.o


CCPLUS = g++


.SUFFIXES: .C .o .h


#
# Program Rules
#


filesys: ${OBJ}
	$(CCPLUS) -o filesys $(OBJ)
#
# Extra dependencies on the header file
# (if the header file changes, we need to rebuild *.o)
#
```

```
cpp-prog.o: filesys.h
X.o: filesys.h
Y.o: filesys.h
Z.o: filesys.h
#
# Suffix rules
#

.C.o:
	$(CCPLUS) -c $<
```

The general rule here tells make that a `.o’ file can be created from a `.C’ file by executing the command `$(CCPLUS) -c’. (This is identical to the C case, except for the name of the compiler). The extra dependencies tell make that, if we change the header file `filesys.h’, then we must recompile all the files which read in `filesys.h’, since this could affect all of these. Finally, the highest level rule says that to make `filesys’ from the `.o’ files, we have to run `$(CCPLUS) -o filesys *.o’.

THE ARGV, ARGC AND ENVP PARAMETERS

When we write C programs which reads command line arguments, they are fed to us as an array of strings called the argument vector. The mechanisms for the C-shell and Perl are derived from the C argument vector. To read in the command line, we write

```
main (argc,argv,envp)
int argc;
char *argv[], *envp[];

{
printf (“The first argument was %s\n”,argv[1]);
}
```

Argument zero is the name of the program itself and `argv[argc-1]’ is the last argument. The above definitions are in Kernighan and Ritchie C style. In ANSI C, the arguments can be declared using prototype:

```
main (int argc, char **argv)

{
```

}

The array of strings `envp[]' is a list of values of the *environment variables* of the system, formatted by

NAME=value

This gives C programmers access to the shell›s global environment.

ENVIRONMENT VARIABLES IN C

In addition to the `envp' vector, it is possible to access the environment variables through the call `getenv()'. This is used as follows; suppose we want to access the shell environment variable `$HOME'.

```
char *string;
string = getenv("HOME");
```

`string' is now a pointer to static but public data. You should not use `string' as if it were you're own property because it will be used again by the system. Copy it's contents to another string before using the data.

```
char buffer[500];
strcpy (buffer,string);
```

FILES AND DIRECTORIES

All of the regular C functions from the standard library are available to UNIX programmers. The standard functions only address the issue of reading and writing to files however, they do not deal with operating system specific attributes such as file permissions and file types. Nor is there a mechanisms for obtaining lists of files within a directory. The reason for these omissions is that they are operating system dependent. To find out about these other attributes POSIX describes some standard UNIX system calls.

opendir, readdir

Files and directories are handled by functions defined in the header file `dirent.h'. In earlier UNIX systems the file `dir.h' was used -- and the definitions were slightly different, but not much. To get a list of files in a directory we must open the directory and read from it -- just like a file. (A directory is just a file which contains data on its entries). The commands are

opendir

closedir

readdir

See the manual pages for dirent. These functions return pointers to a dirent structure which is defined in the file `/usr/include/dirent.h'. Here is an example ls command which lists the contents of the directory `/etc'. This header defines a structure

```
struct dirent
  {
  off_t            d_off;            /* offset of next disk dir entry */
  unsigned long      d_fileno;        /* file number of entry */
  unsigned short     d_reclen;        /* length of this record */
  unsigned short     d_namlen;        /* length of string in d_name */
  char             d_name[255+1];/* name (up to MAXNAMLEN + 1) */
  };
```

which can be used to obtain information from the directory nodes.

```
#include <stdio.h>
#include <dirent.h>
main ()
{ DIR *dirh;
 struct dirent *dirp;
 static char mydir[20] = "/etc";

if ((dirh = opendir(mydir)) == NULL)
  {
  perror("opendir");
  return;
  }

for (dirp = readdir(dirh); dirp != NULL; dirp = readdir(dirh))
  {
  printf("Got dir entry: %s\n",dirp->d_name);
  }

closedir(dirh);
}
```

Notice that reading from a directory is like reading from a file with fgets(), but the entries are filenames rather than lines of text.

stat()

To determine the file properties or *statistics* we use the function call `stat()' or its corollary `lstat()'. Both these functions find out information about files (permissions, owner, filetype etc). The only difference between them is the way in which they treat symbolic links. If `stat' is used on a symbolic link, it stats the file the link points to rather than the link itself. If `lstat' is used, the data refer to the link. Thus, to detect a link, we must use `lstat', See section lstat and readlink.

The data in the `stat› structure are defined in the file `/usr/include/sys/stat.h›. Here are the most important structures.

```
struct    stat
 {
 dev_t      st_dev;          /* device number*/
 ino_t      st_ino;          /* file inode */
 mode_t     st_mode;         /* permission */
 short      st_nlink;        /* Number of hardlinks to file */
 uid_t      st_uid;          /* user id */
 gid_t      st_gid;          /* group id */
 dev_t      st_rdev;
 off_t      st_size;         /* size in bytes */
 time_t     st_atime;        /* time file last accessed */
 time_t     st_mtime;        /* time file contents last modified */
 time_t     st_ctime;        /* time last attribute change */
 long       st_blksize;
 long       st_blocks;
 };
```

lstat and readlink

The function `stat()' treats symbolic links as though they were the files they point to. In other words, if we use `stat()' to read a symbolic link, we end up reading the file the link points to and not the link itself--- we never see symbolic links. To avoid this problem, there is a different version of the stat function called `lstat()' which is identical to `stat()' except that it treats links as links and *not* as the files they point to. This means that we can test whether a file is a symbolic link, only if we use `lstat()'. (See the next paragraph.)

Once we have identified a file to be a symbolic link, we use the `readlink()› function to obtain the name of the file the link points to.

```
#define bufsize 512
char buffer[bufsize];
readlink(«/path/to/file»,buffer,bufsize);
```

The result is returned in the string buffer.

Stat () Test Macros

As we have already mentioned, the UNIX mode bits contain not only information about what permissions a file has, but also bits describing the type of file -- whether it is a directory or a link etc. There are macros defined in UNIX to extract this information from the `st_mode' member of the `stat' structure. They are defined in the `stat.h' headerfile. Here are some examples.

```
#define S_ISBLK(m)   /* is block device */
#define S_ISCHR(m)   /* is character device */
#define S_ISDIR(m)   /* is directory */
#define S_ISFIFO(m)  /* is fifo pipe/socket */
#define S_ISREG(m)   /* is regular (normal) file */
#define S_ISLNK(m)   /* is symbolic link */ /* Not POSIX */
#define S_ISSOCK(m)  /* is a lock */
#define S_IRWXU         /* rwx, owner */
#define         S_IRUSR /* read permission, owner */
#define         S_IWUSR /* write permission, owner */
#define         S_IXUSR         /* execute/search permission, owner */
#define S_IRWXG                 /* rwx, group */
#define         S_IRGRP         /* read permission, group */
#define         S_IWGRP         /* write permission, grougroup */
#define         S_IXGRP         /* execute/search permission, group */
#define S_IRWXO                 /* rwx, other */
#define         S_IROTH         /* read permission, other */
#define         S_IWOTH         /* write permission, other */
#define         S_IXOTH         /* execute/search permission, other */
```

These return true or false when acting on the mode member. Here is an example See section Example filing program.

```
struct stat statvar;
stat("file",&statvar);
/* test return values */
  if (S_ISDIR(statvar.st_mode))
 {
 printf("Is a directory!");
 }
```

Example filing program

The following example program demonstrates the use of the directory functions in dirent and the stat function call.

```
/*****************************************************************/
/*                                                               */
/* Reading directories and `statting' files                      */
/*                                                               */
/*****************************************************************/
#include <stdio.h>
#include <dirent.h>
#include <sys/types.h>
#include <sys/stat.h>
#define DIRNAME "/."
#define bufsize 255
/*****************************************************************/
main ()
{ DIR *dirh;
  struct dirent *dirp;
  struct stat statbuf;
  char *pathname[bufsize];
  char *linkname[bufsize];
if ((dirh = opendir(DIRNAME)) == NULL)
   {
   perror("opendir");
   exit(1);
   }

for (dirp = readdir(dirh); dirp != NULL; dirp = readdir(dirh))
   {
   if (strcmp(".",dirp->d_name) == 0 || strcmp("..",dirp->d_name) == 0)
      {
      continue;
      }
```

```
  if (strcmp("lost+found",dirp->d_name) == 0)
    {
    continue;
    }

  sprintf(pathname,"%s/%s",DIRNAME,dirp->d_name);

  if (lstat(pathname,&statbuf) == -1)          /* see man stat */
   {
   perror("stat");
   continue;
   }

  if (S_ISREG(statbuf.st_mode))
    {
    printf("%s is a regular file\n",pathname);
    };

  if (S_ISDIR(statbuf.st_mode))
    {
    printf("%s is a directory\n",pathname);
    }

  if (S_ISLNK(statbuf.st_mode))
    {
    bzero(linkname,bufsize);                  /* clear string */
    readlink(pathname,linkname,bufsize);
    printf("%s is a link to %s\n",pathname,linkname);
    }

  printf("The mode of %s is %o\n\n",pathname,statbuf.st_mode & 07777);
  }

closedir(dirh);
}
```

PROCESS CONTROL, FORK(), EXEC(), POPEN() AND SYSTEM

There is a number of ways in which processes can interact with one another and in which we can control their behaviour. We shall not go into great detail in this course, only provide examples for reference.

The UNIX `fork()' function is used to create child processes. This is the basis of all `heavyweight' multitasking under UNIX. Here is a simple example of fork in which we start a child process from within a program and wait for it to finish. Note that the code for the parent and the child is is the same file. The only thing that distinguishes parent from child is the value returned by the fork function.

When `fork()' is called, it duplicates the entire current process so that two parallel processes are then running. The only difference between these is that the child process (the copy) gets a return value of zero from `fork()', whereas the parent gets a return value equal to the process identifier (pid) of the child. This value can be used by the parent to send messages or to wait for the child. Here we show a simple example in which the `wait(NULL)' command is used to wait for the last child spawned by the parent.

```
/**********************************************************/
/*                                                        */
/*  A brief demo of the UNIX process duplicator fork().   */
/*                                                        */
/**********************************************************/

#include <stdio.h>

/**********************************************************/

main ()

{ int pid, cid;

pid = getpid();

printf ("Fork demo! I am the parent (pid = %d)\n",pid);

if (! fork())
  {
  cid = getpid();
```

```
  printf ("I am the child (cid = %d) of (pid=%d)\n",cid,pid);
  ChildProcess();
  exit(0);
  }

printf("Parent waiting here for the child...\n");

wait(NULL);

printf("Child finished, parent quitting too!\n");
}

/*************************************************************/

ChildProcess()

{ int i;

for (i = 0; i < 10; i++)
   {
   printf ("%d...\n",i);
   sleep(1);
   }
}
```

Another possibility is that we might want to execute a program and wait to find out what the result of the program is before continuing. There are two ways to do this. The first is a variation on the theme above and uses fork().

Let's create a function which runs a shell command from within a C program, and determines its return value. We make the result a boolean (integer) value, so that the function returns `true' if the shell command exits normally, See section Return codes.

```
    if (ShellCommandReturnsZero(shell-command))
  {
  printf ("Command %s went ok\n",shell-command);
  }
```

To do this we first have to fork a new process and then use one of the exec commands to load a new code image on top of the new process. shell commands from C This sounds complicated, but it is necessary because of the way UNIX handles processes. If we had no use for the return value, we could simply execute a shell command using the system("shell command") function, (which does all this for us) but when system() exits, we can only tell if the command was executed successfully or unsuccessfully--we learn nothing about what actually failed (the shell or command which was executed under the shell?) If we require detailed information about what happened to the child process then we need to do the following.

```
#include <sys/types.h>
#include <sys/wait.h>
 /* Send complete command as a string */
 /* including all arguments         */
    ShellCommandReturnsZero(comm)
char *comm;
{ int status, i, argc;
 pid_t pid;
 char arg[maxshellargs][bufsize];
 char **argv;

/* Build argument array for execv call*/

for (i = 0; i < maxshellargs; i++)
  {
  bzero (arg[i],bufsize);
  }

argc = SplitCommand(comm,arg);

if ((pid = fork()) < 0)
  {
  FatalError("Failed to fork new process");
  }
else if (pid == 0)                /* child */
  {
  argv = malloc((argc+1)*sizeof(char *));
```

```
    for (i = 0; i < argc; i++)
      {
      argv[i] = arg[i];
      }

    argv[i] = (char *) NULL;

    if (execv(arg[0],argv) == -1)
      {
      yyerror("script failed");
      perror("execvp");
      exit(1);
      }
    }
  else                          /* parent */
    {
    if (wait(&status) != pid)
      {
      printf("Wait for child failed\n");
      perror("wait");
      return false;
      }
    else
      {
      if (WIFSIGNALED(status))
        {
        printf("Script %s returned: %s\n",comm,WTERMSIG(status));
        return false;
        }

      if (! WIFEXITED(status))
        {
        return false;
        }
```

```
    if (WEXITSTATUS(status) == 0)
      {
      return true;
      }
    else
      {
      return false;
      }
    }
  }

}

/*****************************************************************/

SplitCommand(comm,arg)

char *comm, arg[maxshellargs][bufsize];

{ char *sp;
 int i = 0, j;
 char buff[bufsize];

for (sp = comm; *sp != NULL; sp++)
  {
  bzero(buff,bufsize);

  if (i >= maxshellargs-1)
    {
    yyerror("Too many arguments in embedded script");
    FatalError("Use a wrapper");
    }
```

```
  while (*sp == ' ' || *sp == '\t')
    {
    sp++;
    }

  switch (*sp)
    {
    case '\"': sscanf (++sp,"%[^\"]",buff);
               break;
    case '\'': sscanf (++sp,"%[^\']",buff);
               break;
    default:   sscanf (sp,"%s",buff);
               break;
    }

  for (j = 0; j < bufsize; j++)
    {
    arg[i][j] = buff[j];
    }

  sp += strlen(arg[i]);
  i++;
  }
return (i);
}
```

In this example, the script waits for the exit signal from the child process before continuing. The return value from the child is available from the wait function with the help of a set of macros defined in `/usr/include/sys/wait.h'. The value is given by WTERMSIG(status).

In the final example, we can open a pipe to a process directly in a C program as though it were a file, by using the function popen(). Pipes may be opened for reading or for writing, in exactly the same way as a file is opened. The child process is automatically synchronized with the parent using this method. Here is a program which opens a UNIX command for reading (both stdout and stderr) from the child process are piped into the program. Notice that the syntax used in this call is that used by the Bourne shell, since this is build deeply into the UNIX execution design.

```
#define bufsize 1024

FILE *pp;
char VBUFF[bufsize];

...

if ((pp = popen( "/sbin/mount -va 2<&1","r")) == NULL)
  {
  printf("Failed to open pipe\n");
  return errorcode;
  }

while (!feof(pp))
  {
  fgets(VBUFF,bufsize,pp);

  /* Just write the output to stdout */

  printf ("Pipe read: %s\n",VBUFF);
  }

pclose(pp);
```

A MORE SECURE POPEN()

One problem with the popen() system call is that it uses a shell to execute the command it obtains a pipe to. In the past this has been used to allow UNIX security breaches, using a so-called IFS attack which can trick the shell into executing a program with the name of the first node in the directory of the executable. For instance,if the pipe was to open the program `/bin/ps', this coudl be tricked into executing a program in the current working directory of the process called `bin' with argument `ps'.

The solution is not to use a shell at all, but to replace popen() with a version which calls exec() directly. Here is a safe version from the source code of cfengine:

```
#define bufsize     4096
#define maxshellargs 20
```

```
pid_t *CHILD;
int   MAXFD = 20; /* Max number of simultaneous pipes */

/***********************************************************/

FILE *cfpopen(command, type)

char *command, *type;

 { char arg[maxshellargs][bufsize];
  int i, argc, pd[2];
  char **argv;
  pid_t pid;
  FILE *pp = NULL;

 if ((*type != 'r' && *type != 'w') || (type[1] != '\0'))
   {
   errno = EINVAL;
   return NULL;
   }

 if (CHILD == NULL)   /* first time */
   {
   if ((CHILD = calloc(MAXFD,sizeof(pid_t))) == NULL)
     {
     return NULL;
     }
   }

 if (pipe(pd) < 0)  /* Create a pair of descriptors to this process */
   {
   return NULL;
   }
```

```
if ((pid = fork()) == -1)
  {
  return NULL;
  }

if (pid == 0)
  {
  switch (*type)
    {
    case 'r':

          close(pd[0]);       /* Don't need output from parent */

          if (pd[1] != 1)
            {
            dup2(pd[1],1);    /* Attach pp=pd[1] to our stdout */
            dup2(pd[1],2);    /* Merge stdout/stderr */
            close(pd[1]);
            }

          break;

    case 'w':

          close(pd[1]);

          if (pd[0] != 0)
            {
            dup2(pd[0],0);
            close(pd[0]);
            }
    }

  for (i = 0; i < MAXFD; i++)
```

```
    {
    if (CHILD[i] > 0)
      {
      close(CHILD[i]);
      }

    argc = SplitCommand(command,arg);
    argv = (char **) malloc((argc+1)*sizeof(char *));

    if (argv == NULL)
      {
      FatalError("Out of memory");
      }

    for (i = 0; i < argc; i++)
      {
      argv[i] = arg[i];
      }

    argv[i] = (char *) NULL;

    if (execv(arg[0],argv) == -1)
      {
      sprintf(OUTPUT,"Couldn't run %s",arg[0]);
      CfLog(cferror,OUTPUT,"execv");
      }

    _exit(1);
    }
  }
else
  {
  switch (*type)
    {
    case 'r':
```

```
            close(pd[1]);

            if ((pp = fdopen(pd[0],type)) == NULL)
              {
              return NULL;
              }
            break;

     case 'w':

            close(pd[0]);

            if ((pp = fdopen(pd[1],type)) == NULL)
              {
              return NULL;
              }
     }

   CHILD[fileno(pp)] = pid;
   return pp;
   }
}

/*************************************************************************/

cfpclose(pp)

FILE *pp;

{ int fd, status;
  pid_t pid;

Debug("cfpclose(pp)\n");
```

```
if (CHILD == NULL)  /* popen hasn't been called */
  {
  return -1;
  }

fd = fileno(pp);

if ((pid = CHILD[fd]) == 0)
  {
  return -1;
  }

CHILD[fd] = 0;

if (fclose(pp) == EOF)
  {
  return -1;
  }

Debug("cfpopen - Waiting for process %d\n",pid);

#ifdef HAVE_WAITPID

while(waitpid(pid,&status,0) < 0)
  {
  if (errno != EINTR)
    {
    return -1;
    }
  }

 return status;

#else
```

```
if (wait(&status) != pid)
  {
  return -1;
  }
else
  {
  if (WIFSIGNALED(status))
    {
    return -1;
    }

  if (! WIFEXITED(status))
    {
    return -1;
    }

  return (WEXITSTATUS(status));
  }
#endif
}

/*****************************************************************/
/* Command exec aids                                          */
/*****************************************************************/

SplitCommand(comm,arg)

char *comm, arg[maxshellargs][bufsize];

{ char *sp;
 int i = 0, j;
 char buff[bufsize];

for (sp = comm; sp < comm+strlen(comm); sp++)
  {
```

```
  bzero(buff,bufsize);

  if (i >= maxshellargs-1)
    {
    CfLog(cferror,"Too many arguments in embedded script","");
    FatalError("Use a wrapper");
    }

  while (*sp == ' ' || *sp == '\t')
    {
    sp++;
    }

  switch (*sp)
    {
    case '\0': return(i-1);

    case '\"': sscanf (++sp,"%[^\"]",arg[i]);
               break;
    case '\'': sscanf (++sp,"%[^\']",arg[i]);
               break;
    case '`':  sscanf (++sp,"%[^`]",arg[i]);
               break;
    default:   sscanf (sp,"%s",arg[i]);
               break;
    }

  sp += strlen(arg[i]);
  i++;
  }

return (i);
}
```

SECTION IV: ADVANCED UNIX PROGRAMMING

4
CHAPTER
ADVANCED UNIX PROGRAMMING

Mark Burgess

TRAPS AND SIGNALS

Processes can receive signals from the UNIX kernel at any time. Some of these signals terminate the execution of the program. This can cause problems if the program is in the middle of critical activity such as writing to a file. For that reason we can trap signals and provide our own routine for handling them in a special way.

A signal handler is made by calling the function `signal()' for each signal and by specifying a pointer to a function which will be called in the event of a signal. For example:

```
main ()

{ int HandleSignal();

signal(SIGTERM,HandleSignal);
}

HandleSignal()

{
/* Tidy up and exit cleanly */
```

Citation: Mark Burgess, Advanced UNIX programming, http://www.iu.hio.no/~mark/unix/unix.html.

```
exit(0);
}
```

`SIGTERM' is the usual signal sent by the command `kill'. There are many other signals which can be sent to programs. Here is list. You have to decide for yourself whether or not you want to provide your own signal handling function. To ignore a signal, you write

```
signal(SIGtype,SIG_IGN);
```

To remove a signal handler and re-activate a signal, you write

```
signal(SIGtype,SIG_DFL);
```

REGULAR EXPRESSIONS

A regular expression is a pattern for matching strings of text. We have met regular expressions earlier in connection with the shell and Perl. Naturally these earlier encounters have their roots in C functions for handling expressions. A regular expression is used by first `compiling' it into a convenient data structure. Then a matching function is used to compare the expression with a test string. In this example program we show how a regular expression typed in as an argument to the program is found within strings of input entered on the keyboard.

```
#include <stdio.h>
#include <regex.h>
main (argc,argv)
int argc;
char **argv;
{
 char buffer[1024];
 regex_t rx;
 regmatch_t match;
 size_t nmatch = 1;
 if (regcomp(&rx, argv[1], REG_EXTENDED) != 0)
   {
   perror("regcomp");
   return;
   }

 while (!feof(stdin))
   {
```

```
  fgets(buffer,1024,stdin);

  if (regexec(&rx,buffer,1,&match,0) == 0)
    {
    printf("Matched:(%s) at %d to %d",buffer,match.rm_so,match.rm_eo);
    }

  }

regfree(&rx);
}
```

Here is an example of its use. The output of the program is in *italics*

% a.out xyz
this is a string
another string
an xyz string
Matched: (an xyz string
) at 3 to 6
another xyz zyxxyz string
Matched: (another xyz xyz string
) at 8 to 11

% a.out 'xyz|abc'
This is a string
An abc string
Matched: (An abc string
) at 3 to 6
Or an xyz string
Matched: (Or an xyz string
) at 6 to 9

If you don't want the match data set &pm to NULL. To get an exact match rather than a substring check that the bounds are 0 and strlen(argv[1])-1.

DES ENCRYPTION

Encryption with the SSLeay library, compile with command

gcc crypto.c -I/usr/local/ssl/include -L/usr/local/ssl/lib -lcrypto

Example of normal triple DES encryption which works only on an 8-byte buffer:

```
/*****************************************************************
*********/
/*                                                   */
/* File: crypto.c                                        */
/*                                                   */
/* Compile with:  gcc program.c  -lcrypto   (SSLeay)                */
/*                                                   */
/*****************************************************************
*********/
#include <stdio.h>
#include <des.h>
\#define bufsize 1024
   /* Note how this truncates to 8 characters */
main ()
{ char in[bufsize],out[bufsize],back[bufsize];
  des_cblock key1,key2,key3,seed = {0xFE,0xDC,0xBA,0x98,0x76,0x54,0x32,0x10};
  des_key_schedule ks1,ks2,ks3;
strcpy(in,"1 2 3 4 5 6 7 8 9 a b c d e f g h i j k");
des_random_seed(seed);
des_random_key(key1);
des_random_key(key2);
des_random_key(key3);
des_set_key((C_Block *)key1,ks1);
des_set_key((C_Block *)key2,ks2);
des_set_key((C_Block *)key3,ks3);
des_ecb3_encrypt((C_Block *)in,(C_Block *)out,ks1,ks2,ks3,DES_ENCRYPT);
printf("Encrypted [%s] into [%s]\n",in,out);
des_ecb3_encrypt((C_Block *)out,(C_Block *)back,ks1,ks2,ks3,DES_DECRYPT);
printf("and back to.. [%s]\n",back);
}
```

Triple DES, chaining mode, for longer strings (which must be a multiple of 8 bytes):

```
/*****************************************************************
*********/
/*                                                              */
/* File: crypto.c                                               */
/*                                                              */
/* Compile with:  gcc program.c  -lcrypto   (SSLeay)            */
/*                                                              */
/*****************************************************************
*********/

#include <stdio.h>
#include <des.h>

#define bufsize 1024

   /* This can be used on arbitrary length buffers */

main ()

{ char in[bufsize],out[bufsize],back[bufsize],workvec[bufsize];
  des_cblock key1,key2,key3,seed = {0xFE,0xDC,0xBA,0x98,0x76,0x54,0x32,0x10};
  des_key_schedule ks1,ks2,ks3;

strcpy(in,"1 2 3 4 5 6 7 8 9 a b c d e f g h i j k l m n o p q r s t u v w x y z");

des_random_seed(seed);

des_random_key(key1);
des_random_key(key2);
des_random_key(key3);

des_set_key((C_Block *)key1,ks1);
des_set_key((C_Block *)key2,ks2);
des_set_key((C_Block *)key3,ks3);
```

```
/* This work vector can be intialized t anything ...*/

memset(workvec,0,bufsize);

des_ede3_cbc_encrypt((C_Block *)in,(C_Block *)out,(long)strlen(in),
        ks1,ks2,ks3,(C_Block *)workvec,DES_ENCRYPT);

printf("Encypted [%s] into [something]\n",in);

/* .. but this must be initialized the same as above */

memset(workvec,0,bufsize);

/* Note that the length is the original length, not strlen(out) */

des_ede3_cbc_encrypt((C_Block *)out,(C_Block *)back,(long)strlen(in),
        ks1,ks2,ks3,(C_Block *)workvec,DES_DECRYPT);

printf("and back to.. [%s]\n",back);
}
```

DEVICE CONTROL: IOCTL

The C function `ioctl' (I/O control) is used to send special control commands to devices like the disk and the network interface. The syntax of the function is

```
int ioctl(fd, request, arg)
int fd, request;
long arg;
```

The first parameter is normally as device handle or socket descriptor. The second is a control parameter. Lists of valid control parameters are normally defined in the system `include' files for a particular device. They are device and system dependent so you need a local manual and som detective work to find out what they are. The final parameter is a pointer to a variable which receives return data from the device.

`ioctl' commands are device specific, by their nature. The commands for the ethernet interface device are only partially standardized, for example. We could read the ethernet device (which is called `le0' on a Sun workstation), using the following command:

```
# include <sys/socket.h>     /* Typical includes for internet */
# include <sys/ioctl.h>
# include <net/if.h>
# include <netinet/in.h>
# include <arpa/inet.h>
# include <netdb.h>
# include <sys/protosw.h>
# include <net/route.h>

struct ifreq IFR;
int sk;
struct sockaddr_in sin;

strcpy(IFR.ifr_name,"le0");
IFR.ifr_addr.sa_family = AF_INET;

if ((sk = socket(AF_INET,SOCK_DGRAM,IPPROTO_IP)) == -1)
  {
  perror("socket");
  exit(1);
  }

if (ioctl(sk,SIOCGIFFLAGS, (caddr_t) &IFR) == -1)
  {
  perror ("ioctl");
  exit(1);
  }
```

We shall not go into the further details of `ioctl', but simply note its role in system programming.

DATABASE EXAMPLE (BERKELEY DB)

```
DBT key,value;
DB *dbp;
```

```
DBC *dbcp;
db_recno_t recno;

if ((errno = db_open(CHECKSUMDB,DB_BTREE, DB_CREATE, 0664, NULL,
NULL, &dbp)) != 0)
  {
  sprintf(OUTPUT,"cfd: couldn't open checksum database %s\n",CHECKSUMDB);
  CfLog(cferror,OUTPUT,"db_open");
  return false;
  }

bzero(&value,sizeof(value));
bzero(&key,sizeof(key));

key.data = filename;
key.size = strlen(filename)+1;
value.data = dbvalue;
value.size = sizeof(dbvalue);

if ((errno = dbp->del(dbp,NULL,&key,0)) != 0)
  {
  CfLog(cferror,"","db_store");
  }

key.data = filename;
key.size = strlen(filename)+1;

if ((errno = dbp->put(dbp,NULL,&key,&value,0)) != 0)
  {
  CfLog(cferror,"put failed","db->put");
  }

if ((errno = dbp->get(dbp,NULL,&key,&value,0)) == 0)
  {
```

```
/* Not found ... */
return;
}

dbp->close(dbp,0);
```

TEXT PARSING TOOLS: `LEX' AND `YACC'

This section is a taster only. You only need to know what lex and yacc are, not how they work.

`lex' and `yacc' are two tools for the C programmer who wishes to make a text parser. A text parser is a program which reads a text file and interprets the symbols in it. Every programming language must include a text parser, for instance.

The `yacc' (yet another compiler compiler) program generates C code which parses a textfile, given a description of the syntax rules for the file. In other words, we define the logical structure of the text file, according to the way we wish to interpret it and give the rules to `yacc'. `yacc' produces C code from this which does the job.

`lex' is a `lexer'. It is normally used together with `yacc'. `lex' *tokenizes* or identifies symbols in a file. What that means is that it reads in a file and matches *types* of string in the file which are defined in terms of regular expressions by the programmer, and returns symbolic values for those strings.

Although `lex› can be used by independently of `yacc›, it is normally used to identify the different *types* of string which define the syntax of a file. For example, suppose `yacc› was parsing a C program. On the beginning of a line, it might expect to find either a variable name or a preprocessor symbol. A variable name is just a string consisting of characters from the set `0-9a-Z_›, whereas a preprocessor command always starts with the character `#›. `yacc› passes control to `lex› which reads the file and matches the first object on the line. If it finds a variable, it returns to `yacc› a *token* which is a number or value corresponding to `variable'. Similarly, if it finds a preprocessor command, it returns a token for that. If it doesn't match either type it returns something else and `yacc› signals a syntax error.

Here is a `yacc› file which parses a file consisting of lines of the form a+b, where a and b are numbers -- any other syntax is incorrect. We could have used this later in the example program for the client-server example, See section Socket streams.

You can learn more about lex and yacc in *"Lex and Yacc", J. Levine, T. Mason and D. Brown, O'Reilly and Assoc.*

```
%{
/*****************************************************************/
/*                                                          */
/*  PARSER for a + b protocol                               */
/*                                                          */
```

```
/* The section between the single %'s gets copied verbatim into    */
/* the resulting C code yacc generates -- including this comment!  */
/*                                                                 */
/*****************************************************************/

#include <stdio.h>

extern char *yytext;

%}

%token NUMBER PLUS

%%

specification:    { yyerror("Warning: invalid statement");}
                  | statement;

statement:        NUMBER PLUS NUMBER;
```

The lexer to go with this parser generates the tokens NUMBER and PLUS used by `yacc':

```
%{
/*****************************************************************/
/*                                                                 */
/*  LEXER for a + b protocol                                       */
/*                                                                 */
/* Returns token types NUMBER and PLUS to yacc, one at a time      */
/*                                                                 */
/*****************************************************************/

#include "y.tab.h"      /* yacc produces this -- need this line! */

%}
```

```
number   [0-9]+
plus     [+]

%%

number          {
            return NUMBER;
            }

plus            {
            return PLUS;
            }

.           {
            return yytext[0];
            }

%%

/* EOF */
```

The main program which uses `yacc' and `lex' looks like this:

```
extern FILE *yyin;
main ()
{
if ((yyin = fopen("My_Input_File","r")) == NULL)     /* Open file */
  {
  printf("Can't open file\n");
  exit (1);
  }

 while (!feof(yyin))
  {
  yyparse();
```

```
  }
fclose (yyin);
}
```

Exercises

1. Write a daemon program with a signal handler which makes a log of the heaviest (maximum cpu) process running, every five minutes. The program should exit if the log file becomes greater than 5-kbytes.
2. Rewrite in C the perl program which lists all the files in the current directory containing a certain string.
3. Write a version of `more' which prints control characters safely. See the `cat -e' command.
4. Write a Makefile to create a shared library from a number of object files.

NETWORK PROGRAMMING

Client-server communication is the basis of modern operating system technology. The UNIX socket mechanism makes stream-based communication virtually transparent.

Socket streams

Analogous to filestreams are *sockets* or TCP/IP *network connections*. A socket is a two-way (read/write) pseudo-file node. An open socket stream is like an open file-descriptor. Berkeley sockets are part of the standard C library.

There are two main kinds of socket: TCP/IP sockets and UNIX domain sockets. UNIX sockets can be used to provide local interprocess communication using a filestream communication protocol. TCP/IP sockets open file descriptors across the network. A TCP/IP socket is a file stream associated with an IP address and a port number. We write to a socket descriptor just as with a file descriptor, either with write() or using send().

When sending binary data over a network we have to be careful about machine level representations of data. Operating systems (actually the hardware they run on) fall into two categories known as *big endian* and *little endian*. The names refer to the *byte-order* of numerical representations. The names indicate how large integers (which require say 32 bits or more) are stored in memory. Little endian systems store the least significant byte first, while big endian systems store the most significant byte first. For example, the representation of the number 34,677,374 has either of these forms.

```
             ----------------------------------
Big       |  2     |  17    |  34     |  126   |
             ----------------------------------

             ----------------------------------
Little    |  126   |  34    |  17     |  2     |
             ----------------------------------
```

Obviously if we are transferring data from one host to another, both hosts have to agree on the data representation otherwise there would be disastrous consequences. This means that there has to be a common standard of *network byte ordering*. For example, Solaris (SPARC hardware) uses network byte ordering (big endian), while GNU/Linux (Intel hardware) uses the opposite (little endian). This means that Intel systems have to convert the format every time something is transmitted over the network. UNIX systems provide generic functions for converting between host-byteorder and network-byteorder for small and long integer data:

htonl, htons, ntohl, ntohs

Here we list two example programs which show how to make a client-server pair. The server enters a loop, and listens for connections from any clients (the generic address `INADDR_ANY' is a wildcard for any address on the current local network segment). The client program sends requests to the server as a protocol in the form of a string of the type `a + b'. Normally `a' and `b' are numbers, in which case the server returns their sum to the client. If the message has the special form `halt + *', where the star is arbitrary, then the server shuts down. Any other form of message results in an error, which the server signals to the client.

The basic structure of the client-server components in terms of system calls is this:

Client:

```
socket()      Create a socket
connect()     Contact a server socket (IP + port)

  while (?)
    {
    send()    Send to server
    recv()    Receive from server
    }
```

Server:

```
socket()      Create a socket
bind()        Associates the socket with a fixed address
listen()      Create a listen queue

while()
  {
```

```
reply=accept()  Accept a connection request
recv()          Receive from client
send()          Send to client
}

/*******************************************************************
**/
/*                                               */
/* The client part of a client-server pair. This simply takes two    */
/* numbers and adds them together, returning the result to the client */
/*                                               */
/* Compiled with:                                      */
/*              cc server.c                        */
/*                                               */
/* User types:                                     */
/*              3 + 5                             */
/*              a + b                             */
/*              halt + server                        */
/*******************************************************************
**/

#include <stdio.h>
#include <sys/types.h>
#include <sys/socket.h>
#include <netinet/in.h>
#include <netdb.h>

#define PORT 9000             /* Arbitrary non-reserved port */
#define HOST "nexus.iu.hio.no"
#define bufsize 20

/*******************************************************************
**/
/* Main                                          */
/*******************************************************************
**/
```

```
main (argc,argv)

int argc;
char *argv[];

{ struct sockaddr_in cin;
  struct hostent *hp;
  char buffer[bufsize];
  int sd;

if (argc != 4)
   {
   printf("syntax: client a + b\n");
   exit(1);
   }

if ((hp = gethostbyname(HOST)) == NULL)
   {
   perror("gethostbyname: ");
   exit(1);
   }

memset(&cin,0,sizeof(cin));          /* Another way to zero memory */

cin.sin_family = AF_INET;
cin.sin_addr.s_addr = ((struct in_addr *)(hp->h_addr))->s_addr;
cin.sin_port = htons(PORT);

printf("Trying to connect to %s = %s\n",HOST,inet_ntoa(cin.sin_addr));

if ((sd = socket(AF_INET,SOCK_STREAM,0)) == -1)
   {
   perror("socket");
```

```
  exit(1);
  }

if (connect(sd,&cin,sizeof(cin)) == -1)
  {
  perror("connect");
  exit(1);
  }

sprintf(buffer,"%s + %s",argv[1],argv[3]);

if (send(sd,buffer,strlen(buffer),0) == -1)
  {
  perror ("send");
  exit(1);
  }

if (recv(sd,buffer,bufsize,0) == -1)
  {
  perror("recv");
  exit (1);
  }

printf ("Server responded with %s\n",buffer);

close (sd);
unlink("./socket");
}

/*****************************************************************
**/
/*                                                              */
/* The server part of a client-server pair. This simply takes two    */
/* numbers and adds them together, returning the result to the client */
/*                                                              */
```

```
/* Compiled with:                                    */
/*              cc server.c                          */
/*                                                   */
/*****************************************************************
**/

#include <stdio.h>
#include <sys/types.h>
#include <sys/socket.h>
#include <netinet/in.h>
#include <netdb.h>

#define PORT 9000
#define bufsize 20
#define queuesize 5
#define true 1
#define false 0

/*****************************************************************
**/
/* Main                                              */
/*****************************************************************
**/

main ()

{ struct sockaddr_in cin;
  struct sockaddr_in sin;
  struct hostent *hp;
  char buffer[bufsize];
  int sd, sd_client, addrlen;

memset(&sin,0,sizeof(sin));      /* Another way to zero memory */
sin.sin_family = AF_INET;
sin.sin_addr.s_addr = INADDR_ANY;        /* Broadcast address */
sin.sin_port = htons(PORT);
```

```
if ((sd = socket(AF_INET,SOCK_STREAM,0)) == -1)
  {
  perror("socket");
  exit(1);
  }

if (bind(sd,&sin,sizeof(sin)) == -1)  /* Must have this on server */
  {
  perror("bind");
  exit(1);
  }

if (listen(sd,queuesize) == -1)
  {
  perror("listen");
  exit(1);
  }

while (true)
 {
 if ((sd_client = accept(sd,&cin,&addrlen)) == -1)
    {
    perror("accept");
    exit(1);
    }

  if (recv(sd_client,buffer,sizeof(buffer),0) == -1)
    {
    perror("recv");
    exit(1);
    }

  if (!DoService(buffer))
    {
```

```
    break;
    }

  if (send(sd_client,buffer,strlen(buffer),0) == -1)
    {
    perror("send");
    exit(1);
    }

  close (sd_client);
  }

close (sd);
printf("Server closing down...\n");
}

/**************************************************************/

DoService(buffer)

char *buffer;

 /* This is the protocol section. Here we must */
 /* check that the incoming data are sensible  */

{ int a=0,b=0;

printf("Received: %s\n",buffer);
sscanf(buffer,"%d + %d\n",&a,&b);

if (a > 0 && b> 0)
  {
  sprintf(buffer,"%d + %d = %d",a,b,a+b);
  return true;
  }
```

```
else
 {
 if (strncmp("halt",buffer,4) == 0)
   {
   sprintf(buffer,"Server closing down!");
   return false;
   }
 else
   {
   sprintf(buffer,"Invalid protocol");
   return true;
   }
 }
}
```

In the example we use `streams' to implement a typical input/output behaviour for C. A stream interface is a so-called reliable protocol. There are other kinds of sockets too, called *unrealiable*, or UDP sockets. Features to notice on the server are that we must bind to a specific address. The client is always implicitly bound to an address since a socket connection always originates from the machine on which the client is running. On the server however we want to know which addresses we shall be receiving requests from. In the above example we use the generic wildcard address `INADDR_ ANY' which means that any host can connect to the server. Had we been more specific, we could have limited communication to two machines only.

By calling `listen()' we set up a queue for incoming connections. Rather than forking a separate process to handle each request we set up a queue of a certain depth. If we exceed this depth then new clients rtying to connect will be refused connection.

The `accept' call is the mechanism which extracts a `reply handle' from the socket. Using the handle obtained from this call we can reply to the client without having to open a special socket explicitly.

An improved server side connection can be setup, reading the service name from `/ etc/services' and setting reusable socket options to avoid busy signals, like this:

```
struct sockaddr_in cin, sin;
struct servent *server;
int sd, addrlen = sizeof(cin);
int portnumber, yes=1;
if ((server = getservbyname(service-name,"tcp")) == NULL)
   {
```

```
   CfLog(cferror,"Couldn't get cfengine service","getservbyname");
   exit (1);
   }

 bzero(&cin,sizeof(cin));

/* Service returns network byte order */

 sin.sin_port = (unsigned short)(server->s_port);
 sin.sin_addr.s_addr = INADDR_ANY;
 sin.sin_family = AF_INET;

 if ((sd = socket(AF_INET,SOCK_STREAM,0)) == -1)
   {
   CfLog(cferror,"Couldn't open socket","socket");
   exit (1);
   }

 if (setsockopt (sd, SOL_SOCKET, SO_REUSEADDR,
             (char *) &yes, sizeof (int)) == -1)
   {
   CfLog(cferror,"Couldn't set socket options","sockopt");
   exit (1);
   }


 if (bind(sd,(struct sockaddr *)&sin,sizeof(sin)) == -1)
   {

   }

/* etc */
```

MULTITHREADING A SERVER

All the arguments must be collected into a struct, since only one argument pointer can be sent to the pthread functions.

```
#include <pthread.h>
     SpawnCfGetFile(args)
struct cfd_thread_arg *args;
{ pthread_t tid;
 void *CfGetFile();
pthread_attr_init(&PTHREADDEFAULTS);
pthread_attr_setdetachstate(&PTHREADDEFAULTS,PTHREAD_CREATE_
DETACHED);

if (pthread_create(&tid,&PTHREADDEFAULTS,CfGetFile,args) != 0)
  {
  CfLog(cferror,"pthread_create failed","create");
  CfGetFile(args);
  }

pthread_attr_destroy(&PTHREADDEFAULTS);
}
/*************************************************************/
void *CfGetFile(args)
\struct cfd_thread_arg *args;

{ pthread_mutex_t mutex;

if (pthread_mutex_lock(&mutex) != 0)
  {
  CfLog(cferror,"pthread_mutex_lock failed","pthread_mutex_lock");
  free(args->replyfile);  /* from strdup in each thread */
  DeleteConn(args->connect);
  free((char *)args);
  return NULL;
  }
```

```
ACTIVE_THREADS++;  /* Global variable */

if (pthread_mutex_unlock(&mutex) != 0)
  {
  CfLog(cferror,"pthread_mutex_unlock failed","unlock");
  }


 /* send data */

if (pthread_mutex_lock(&mutex) != 0)
  {
  CfLog(cferror,"pthread_mutex_lock failed","pthread_mutex_lock");
  return;
  }

ACTIVE_THREADS--;

if (pthread_mutex_unlock(&mutex) != 0)
  {
  CfLog(cferror,"pthread_mutex_unlock failed","unlock");
  }

#endif

return NULL;
}
```

SYSTEM DATABASES

The C library calls which query the databases are, amongst others,

getpwnam *get password data by name*

getpwuid *get password data by uid*

getgrnam *get group data by name*

gethostent *get entry in hosts database*

getnetgrent *get entry in netgroups database*

getservbyname *get servive by name*

getservbyport *get service by port*

get protobyname *get protocol by name*

For a complete list and how to use these, see the UNIX manual.

The following example shows how to read the password file of the system. The functions used here can be used regardless of whether the network information service (NIS) is in use. The data are returned in a structure which is defined in `/usr/include/pwd.h'.

```
/*****************************************************************/
/*                                                       */
/* Read the passwd file by name and sequentially                  */
/*                                                       */
/*****************************************************************/

#include <unistd.h>
#include <pwd.h>

main ()

{ uid_t uid;
  struct passwd *pw;

uid = getuid();

pw = getpwuid(uid);

printf ("Your login name is %s\n",pw->pw_name);

printf ("Now here comes the whole file!\n\n");

setpwent();

while (getpwent())
  {
```

```
  printf ("%s:%s:%s\n",pw->pw_name,pw->pw_gecos,pw->pw_dir);
  }

endpwent();
}
```

DNS - THE DOMAIN NAME SERVICE

The second network database service is that which converts host and domain names into IP numbers and vice versa. This is the domain name service, usually implemented by the BIND (Berkeley Internet Name Domain) software. The information here concerns version 4.9 of this software.

gethostbyname()

This is perhaps the most important function form hostname lookup. `gethostbyname()' gets its information either from files, NIS or DNS. Its behaviour is configured by the files mentioned above, See section DNS - The Domain Name Service. It is used to look up the IP address of a named host (including domain name if DNS is used). On the configurable systems described above, the full list of servers is queried until a reply is obtained. The order in which the different services are queried is important here since DNS returns a *fully qualified name* (host name plus domain name) whereas NIS and the `/etc/hosts› file database return only a hostname.

gethostbyname returns data in the form of a pointer to a static data structure. The syntax is

```
#include <netdb.h>
struct hostent *hp;
hp = gethostbyname(«myhost.domain.country»)
```

The resulting structure varies on different implementations of UNIX, but the `old BSD standard› is of the form:

```
struct  hostent
  {
  char   *h_name;       /* official name of host */
  char   **h_aliases;   /* alias list */
  int    h_addrtype;    /* host address type */
  int    h_length;      /* length of address */
  char   **h_addr_list; /* list of addresses from name server */
  };

#define h_addr  h_addr_list[0]  /* address, for backward compatiblity */
```

The structure contains a list of addresses and or aliases from the nameserver. The interesting quantity is usually extracted by means of the macro `h_addr› whcih gives the first value in the address list, though officially one should examine the whole list now.

This value is a pointer which can be converted into a text form by the following hideous type transformation:

```
#include <sys/types.h>
#include <sys/socket.h>
#include <netinet/in.h>
struct sockaddr_in sin;
\cin.sin_addr.s_addr = ((struct in_addr *)(hp->h_addr))->s_addr;
printf(«IP address = %s\n»,inet_ntoa(cin.sin_addr));
```

See the client program in the first section of this chapter for an example of its use.

C SUPPORT FOR NFS

The support for NFS mounting in the standard C library is through two sources. NFS is based on the Sun's RPC system, so the basic calls are only instances of standard RPC protocols.

The C functions in the standard input/output library can be used to access NFS filesystems. Since NFS imitates the UNIX filesystem as closely as possible, NFS filesystems can be mounted in exactly the same way as ordinary filesystems. Unfortunately, the C functions which perform the mount operation in UNIX and depressingly non-standard. They differ on almost every implementation of UNIX.

The basic function which mounts a filesystem, in `mount' (see man (2) mount). The mount table is stored in a file */etc/mtab* on BSD systems (again the name varies wildly from UNIX to UNIX, mnttab on HPUX for instance). The file */etc/rmtab* on an NFS server contains a list of remote-mounted filesystems which are mounted by remote clients. C functions exist which can read the filesystem tables and place the resulting data in C struct types. Alas, these struct defintions are also quite different on different systems. See `/usr/include/sys/mount.h›, so the user wishing to write system-independent code is confounded at the lowest level.

Exercises

- Use `gethostbyname()' to make a simple program like `nslookup' which gives the internet address of a named host.
- Modify the client server example above to make a `remote ls' command called `rls'. You should be able to use the syntax
- rls (options) hostname:/path/to/file

SUMMARY OF PROGRAMMING IDIOMS.

True and false

C shell

True - non-zero/non-empty value
False - zero or null string

Bourne shell

True - 0 returned by shell command
False - non-zero returned by shell command

(Note that "test" converts from C shell style to Bourne shell)

Perl

True - non-zero/non-empty value
False - zero or null string

/* C */

True - non zero integer
False - zero integer

Input from tty

C shell

$<

Bourne shell

line
read

Perl

```
  <STDIN>

/* C */

  scanf
```

Redirection of I/O

```
# C  shell

  command >  file
  command >& file
  command >> file
  command1 |  command2

# Bourne shell

  command > file
  command > file 2>&1
  command >> file
  command1 | command2

# Perl

  open (HANDLE,">file")
  open (HANDLE,">file 2>&1")
  open (HANDLE,">>file")
  open (HANDLE,"command1 |")
  open (HANDLE,"| command2")

/* C */

  fopen ("file","w"); printf(..)
  fopen ("file","w"); printf(..); fprintf(stderr,..)
```

```
fopen ("file","a"); printf(..)
popen ("command1","r")
popen ("command2","w")
```

Loops and tests

```
/* C */ Shell

 foreach end        if then else endif
 while end          switch case breaksw endsw
 repeat

# Bourne shell

 while do done      if then else fi
 until do done      case in esac
 for in do done

# Perl

 while              if then else
 for                unless else
 foreach
 until
 do while
 do until

/* C */

 while              if then else
 do while           switch case
 for
```

Arguments from command line

```
# C shell
```

```
  $argv[]
  $#argv

# Bourne Shell

  $1, $2, $3...  $*
  $#

# Perl

  $ARGV[]
  $#ARGV

/* C */

  char argv[][]
  int  argc
```

Arithmetic

```
# C shell

   a = $b + $c

# Bourne shell

  a = `expr $b + $c`

# Perl

  $a = $b + $c;

/* C */

  a = b + c;
```

Numerical comparison

```
# C shell

  if ( $x == $y ) then
  endif

# Bourne shell

  if [ $x -eq $y ]; then
  fi

# Perl

  if ( $x == $y )
    {
    }

/* C */

  if ( x == y )
    {
    }
```

String comparison

```
# C shell

  if ( $x == $y ) then
  endif

# Bourne shell

  if [ $x = $y ]; then
  fi
```

Perl

```
  if ( $x eq $y ) then
    {
    }
```

/* C */

```
  if (strcmp(x,y) == 0)
    {
    }
```

Opening a file

C shell, Bourne shell - cannot be done (pipes only)

Perl

```
  open (READ_HANDLE,"filename");
  open (WRITE_HANDLE,"> filename");
  open (APPEND_HANDLE,">> filename");
```

/* C */

```
  FILE *fp;

  fp = fopen ("file","r");
  fp = fopen ("file","w");
  fp = fopen ("file","a");
```

Opening a directory

C shell

```
  foreach dir ( directory/* )
```

```
   ...
  end

# Bourne shell

  for dir in directory/* ;
  do
   ...
  done

# Perl

  opendir (HANDLE,"directory") || die;

  while ($entry = readdir(HANDLE))
    {
    }

  closedir(HANDLE);

# C

  #include <dirent.h>
  DIR *dirh;
  struct dirent *dirp;

  if ((dirh = opendir(name)) == NULL)
    {
    perror("opendir")
    exit(1);
    }

  for (dirp = readdir(dirh); dirp != NULL; dirp = readdir(dirh))
    {
    ... /* dirp->d_name points to child */
```

```
  }

 closedir(dirh);
```

Testing file types

```
# C shell

   if ( -f file )  # plain file
   if ( -d file )  # directory

# Bourne shell

   if [ -f file ]  # plain file
   if [ -d file ]  # directory

# Perl

   if ( -f file )  # plain file
   if ( -d file )  # directory
   if ( -l file )  # symbolic link

/* C */

    #include <sys/stat.h>

    struct stat statvar;

    stat("file", &statvar);

    if (S_ISREG(statvar.mode))  /* plain file */
    if (S_ISDIR(statvar.mode))  /* directory  */

    lstat("file", &statvar);
```

```
if (S_ISLNK(statvar.mode))  /* symbolic link */
```

COMMAND AND VARIABLE INDEX

CONCEPT INDEX

INDEX